FROM GRIEF TO GROWTH

5 ESSENTIAL ELEMENTS OF ACTION TO GIVE GRIEF PURPOSE AND GROW FROM YOUR EXPERIENCE

PAULA STEPHENS, MA

Printed in the United States of America

First Printing, 2016

ISBN 978-0-9982489-1-2

www.crazygoodgrief.com

TABLE OF CONTENTS

INTRODUCTION 5

CHAPTER 1—PERSONIFY YOUR GRIEF 27

CHAPTER 2—ELEMENT: WELLNESS AND SELF-CARE 51

CHAPTER 3—ELEMENT: LETTING GO OF
LIMITING BELIEFS 81

CHAPTER 4—ELEMENT: LOVING SELF AND OTHERS.......103

CHAPTER 5—ELEMENT: CREATING CONNECTIONS
THAT HEAL 121

CHAPTER 6—ELEMENT: GRATITUDE 147

CHAPTER 7—FINDING YOUR EMPOWERED PURPOSE......163

ACKNOWLEDGMENTS 175

ABOUT THE AUTHOR 179

END NOTES 181

INTRODUCTION

"The wound is the place where the Light enters you."

—Rumi[1]

Grief, loss, and I have had a long-standing relationship that goes back to my high school years. I guess you could say grief is my high school sweetheart.

I remember learning about Elisabeth Kübler-Ross' Five Stages of Grief[2] in my high school psychology class. It is the stages with which many of us are quite familiar. They are:

1. Denial

2. Bargaining

3. Anger

4. Depression

5. Acceptance

As we were learning about grief, that happened to be the semester my father died after a long battle with cancer. I felt especially uncomfortable in class, like all eyes were on me. I was actually experiencing grief in those moments we were learning about it. I was the only person who could even begin to have an understanding of such a deep topic at the young age of 16. I also remember feeling relief, thinking—if only for a flash of a teenage second—that maybe I wasn't crazy for how I had been feeling.

But as is the case with grief, I couldn't stand it anymore. So promptly after class that day, I ditched the rest of school and got completely drunk. Evidence, perhaps, that I was still in the Anger stage of grief, sprinkled with some Denial.

Looking back now, I can see a direct correlation to the progression of my father's cancer and the progression of my own delinquent behavior. You see, anticipatory grief can start even before death. When we know our loved one is going to die, we tend to start the grief process earlier.

With my mom consumed with my father's day-to-day care, as she should have been, I was pretty much left to my own devices of figuring out how to manage this situation, for which no teenager is equipped. And so in the last two years before my father died, I moved between anger and denial frequently.

When I was angry I would drink, smoke, fight, and find other ways to break the law and purposefully challenge my own mortality. Next, when I was struggling with denial I would drink, smoke, fight, find other ways to break the law, and purposefully challenge my own mortality—sound familiar?

And so, due to grief, I self-medicated through the first two and half years of high school, which my attendance or lack of attendance shows. Fortunately for me, all my records were expunged when I turned 18—even the vehicular assault on a police officer. But you didn't hear that from me.

Then after those years of starting the grieving process for a father who would die, a funny thing happened on a Christmas Eve morning. That was the day my Dad told his doctors to stop doing anything for him—he was ready to let go. He basically told them it was time to die. His declaration was his last gift to me.

I had found Acceptance.

That Christmas Eve morning felt like someone had turned off the buzz of energy that had been created around knowing and waiting for this day to come. Although in the years leading up to that day, we never talked about—not once—that cancer would end my dad's life. So when the time actually came, it felt so strange. My mind and body got quiet.

Before, even with all my self-medicating and risk-taking behavior, I couldn't quiet the harsh truth that the death of my father was always imminent. I couldn't get away from living in anger and denial. But now, knowing that today would be my dad's last day on earth, I no longer had to choose between anger and denial. Acceptance was the only choice.

Somehow, when it's our only choice, we find the finality in it. We realize we have no control. With acceptance as the only option, we finally choose it, though all along we could have chosen it.

While I had gone through all of the Five Stages of Grief during my dad's illness and death, there was so much more going on emotionally that I didn't realize. But like so many, I just didn't know what this grief thing was, or how to deal with it.

It would be 20-plus years of acceptance and a long overstayed visit from my old friend anger before I would seek to discover a deeper, more meaningful way of living a fulfilling life after loss. It would also be a result of additional losses, greater than the loss of my father.

Tough Love

In early April of 2007, my "typical" life as a single mom of three teenage boys would invite another lesson in grief and loss. And by typical I mean that we as a family have never fit nicely into the box of "Average Suburban American Family." My three boys—Brandon, Daniel, and Jason—were hardwired to be like Tom Sawyer and Huckleberry Finn, with a little Dennis the Menace and Lewis and Clark thrown in. It was chaos.

Our atypical lives took on a new twist when Daniel, who was only 14, left for school one morning. By that evening we would realize he had never attended school that day, but had instead run away. The similarities between myself at that age and Daniel were not lost on me.

When he showed up ten days later he was tired, dirty, skinny, incoherent and exhausted from days over-abusing whatever drugs he put in his body. Throughout the entire ten days, though terrified, in my heart I knew that Daniel would return; hope guaranteed that I knew I would see my son again. Hope seemed to be all I had at times. And as a mother, you hang onto hope as hard as you can.

A month later, I made the decision that on the day after his 15th birthday, I would put him on an airplane to a therapy center in Hawaii. Now, Hawaii is a beautiful place to visit. But when you're an angry 15-year-old boy in lock down, having to ring a bell while you're doing your business in an outhouse so they know you haven't run away, it's not a vacation. From there he went to boarding school in northern Montana. It shouldn't have been a surprise two months later when I got the call from the school that Daniel had run away—again. The school said flatly that if/ when he was found, he could not return.

Our lives seemed to be tumbling out of control. Jason was at that tender middle school age, and having a brother in rehab certainly didn't make life any easier. But as had become his role in the family, he worked hard to counter his brother's chaos by being the good kid. From the outside, Jason seemed to be handling things just fine by taking on this role of the hero child. But our outsides usually don't show what is happening on the inside.

The truth was that Daniel, older by only 13 months, had always been Jason's best friend and North Star. Inside, Jason was being torn apart by what was happening to his family.

Brandon reacted differently to what was going on; he actually withdrew and disconnected. Looking back, I think he felt guilty, as if he'd failed Daniel as a big brother.

I contacted the consultant I was using to help guide me through this horrible process. I needed help and advice. I was no longer the parent trying to navigate homecoming dances and driving lessons. I was now the parent running a command center that included hired thugs to find my son and secure him in a cheap hotel room in Idaho. I felt helpless. I felt like a total failure as a mother.

After listening to the various options, I decided to send Daniel back into a tougher wilderness therapy program. By "tough," I mean the kids backpacked five to ten miles a day and lived a very primitive lifestyle. They were led by incredible outdoor guides who loved these kids who were unable to love themselves. But it was tough love. For example, if you wanted warm food, you'd better make a friend and ask them to teach you how to build a fire. Want a spoon? Learn to make do with a stick.

On his third week there, the therapist called to say said it had rained all week and the kids were muddy, wet, and cold most of the week. My heart sank for my boy. But when I asked how he was, the therapist chuckled and said the worse things got, the better Daniel responded. Putting him in the wilderness was like throwing Brer Rabbit in the briar patch! To this day, Daniel is most at peace in the wilderness.

Sometimes, what we need most is a tough situation to give us some perspective. Somehow, it makes us feel completely alive in ways we never imagined.

After 15 months, four states, two bodyguards, and collecting therapists like baseball cards, my three boys and I would be a family again. I always knew he would come back and we always had hope. We were survivors.

Never in my wildest dreams would I have thought our family would go through an experience like we had with Daniel. At times it felt like a made-for-TV movie. But, life returned to "normal" and I felt confident our family would never again experience any greater upheaval than what we'd already been through.

GRIEF COMES AGAIN

In October of 2010, my oldest son Brandon was graduating from Army basic training in Ft. Benning, Georgia. I was so proud of him for joining the Army and being willing to serve our country. He excelled in that environment much like Daniel had excelled in the wilderness. It felt like such a time of celebration. At the time, Daniel was away at college, so Jason and I flew down to Georgia for Brandon's basic training graduation. It would be a long day of travel and sitting in airports and on planes, so I went out for a morning run before we left town.

The dirt was soft under my feet and the October morning air was crisp. As always happens on my runs, the anxiety that had been a part of life since Daniel ran away began to soften. As I reflected back on the last three years, I could see that we, as a family, had come so far. Daniel had graduated from high school. Jason excelled as the leader on his high school lacrosse team and was finding his own identity without the burden of his family's dysfunction.

Then there was Brandon, who found his calling in the military. As a little boy, Brandon would spend hours making forts and playing Army with his friends. For Halloween, if he wasn't dressed to scare, he was dressed in some type of military uniform. My favorite was his fighter pilot suit he bought at the Army Surplus Store and wore in sixth grade when most of his classmates were outgrowing playing dress up at Halloween. My all-time favorite picture of Brandon is one taken on Christmas Eve when he was 13, dressed in my Dad's World War II uniform.

But I think what really moved Brandon to make the decision to join the Army was his budding relationship with my new husband, Scott. Scott had been in the Army and served in Iraq. This was exactly the influence Brandon needed to bring his boyhood dreams of being a solider to life.

Our family had changed so much, including adding boy number four to my collection. With my new husband, we had Sam, who was now just over two years old. We had all worked so hard, each of us in our own way, and it was finally paying off. On that run that morning before flying out, I was just happy.

During the last three years I had been a faithful student of the lessons the Divine was giving me. I had not winced, wavered, or shrunk from any of it. I felt the time had come for me to accept something greater than myself had given me opportunities to learn what's really important in life. Now it was time for me to take these lessons and move forward with them, not continue to live in fear.

At the heart of these lessons was what Daniel had shown us in the wilderness. The harder things are and the more it hurts, the more we need to lean in to those places because they will yield the greatest return on the investment in ourselves, our lives, our relationships, and the joy we feel every day. I made a conscious decision on that morning run to stop waiting for the other shoe to drop and allow myself to feel the abundant joy in my life. After all, I had worked hard for the life I had. It would be a choice that would haunt me and pitch me back into the depths of anger. For the next two years I would blame myself, believing that because I let my guard down I had somehow invited an awful thing to happen to my family.

And just like that, our world changed.

On the morning of October 9, 2010, I got the news that lives in the fearful dark shadows of every parent's worst nightmare. The statement that, when other parents hear it's happened to you, they say, "I could never survive that." And what they actually mean is, "I'm glad it's you and not me."

"This" was the wound that people don't heal from. "This" was every parent's worst nightmare. "This" was what people whisper about because it's too painful to say out loud. "This" is an event that creates a title for which there is no word in the English language. "This" was the death of a child. But not a child as reported by the dry 5 o'clock news anchor that you can disconnect from by flipping the channel.

"This" was *my* child.

13

PAULA STEPHENS, MA

My oldest son, Brandon, died on October 9, 2010, from an accidental overdose while home on leave from the Army.

When Daniel had been gone and had run away, I always knew he'd come home alive and always had hope. But that hope could not help me now. This time, there was no coming home and there was no hope of seeing Brandon alive ever again.

As many teenagers do, Brandon had experimented with drugs and alcohol, but since joining the Army this was not a part of this life. The irony of Brandon's accidental overdose was that it was from half a prescription pain killer. Yes, you read that correctly, *half a pill*. The coroner reported he had never seen a death like this. There was only the one substance in the toxicology report—no alcohol or anything else—and the levels were hardly fatal. The best explanation the coroner could give was that the pill Brandon took was an extended release tablet. When he broke the pill, it changed the chemical structure of the medication. So instead of releasing over an eight hour period, it dumped into his system all at once, causing an overdose. Obviously someone who is a drug addict doesn't take half a pill.

The gentleman investigating his death said it was a case of a perfect storm. Brandon took the pill on an empty stomach and wasn't a drug addict, so he had no tolerance to the medication and none of the people he was with considered taking him to the hospital when he unexpectedly fell asleep on the couch early in the evening. Had any one of those variables been different, Brandon would be here today.

This was such a stark contrast to the vast amount and types of drugs Daniel took. There was an absurd irony about the fact that Daniel should've died many times over from all the drugs he took, and Brandon only took half a pill and died in his sleep. This became a very hard thing for Daniel to reconcile. He struggled with this for a long time in his grieving process. It was also very hard for me to resolve in my mind. How could we be a family that had done so much work and be blindsided by such a freak accident?

I arrived on the scene in time to see Brandon, lifeless, covered with a sheet up to his neck, on a stretcher. It is a moment in time I will never forget. I touched all the spots on his face I wanted to burn into my memory. His full lips, high cheek bones, thick eyebrows, the cow-lick that punctuated his hairline, and most memorable was the perfect circle chicken pox scar in the middle of his forehead from when he was four.

I can look back now and see how the death of my father and the death of Brandon both contained the stages of grief, but the death of my son truly shattered my life into unrecognizable pieces that I doubted could ever be rebuilt. With my father's death, even if I didn't know it and we as a family didn't acknowledge it, there were many years of anticipatory grief before he actually passed away. While it doesn't erase the pain, it does alter it somewhat. Cancer, while awful, is something people recognize and can begin to process.

On the other hand, the death of a child is considered to be an "out of order" death. We assume we will outlive our parents, but it's not in the natural order to outlive our children. One of my many ah-ha's in early grief was there is no word in English, or any other language, to identify someone who has lost a child. We use words like orphan or widow to identify the loss of parents or a spouse. The closest we come is in a word from the ancient language of Sanskrit, "Vilomah," which translates to "out of the natural order."

More importantly than being able to put a label on a loss is the recognition that all losses are hard because they disrupt our belief about how our lives are *supposed* to be. As painful as both of these losses were for me, the ultimate result, and the one I hope you learn to embody through the elements in this book, is that death and loss are the ultimate reminders to live our one wild and precious life fully.

In the weeks that followed Brandon's death, I would flip back through the mental pages of the last three years, looking at every detail. We had made it through so much as a family, only to arrive here. In the 15 months Daniel was in rehab, the three boys and I had each worked on our own baggage that created dysfunction in our family. We had come together and worked on healing wounds that went back to when I had divorced their father years earlier. I was so proud of these young men, having done the type of work that was asked of them at such a young age.

We had already paid our dues, we had done the hard work and we should have been reaping the benefit of our labors. What had I missed? Where did we zig when we should've zagged?

GRIEF IS NOT FLAT

I wish Brandon were here. I miss him every day. I wish so much that things could have been different. I know his absence has changed us in ways beyond our own comprehension. As you go through grief, the "what ifs" will plague you, if you let them.

At some point, I did reach Acceptance. I also learned a lot of other things I didn't realize in my first go-around with grief as a teenager. If I have to live without my soulful, wear-your-heart-on-your-sleeve soldier-boy, then I take comfort in the lessons I've learned because of his death. That is my hope now.

As parents, we think it's our job to teach our children the ways of the world, but I have learned so much more about life from what my boys have taught me than I could have ever taught them. They've shown me what's important and how to bare your soul without losing it. They've also taught me the amazing transformation that happens when you rise from the ashes. My boys raised a good mama.

In my life after losing Brandon, I've become a voice for grief and loss. I speak and consult and offer retreats to help those who are in the middle of it. I've devoted time and energy into helping others face grief and navigate their way through it. I've learned that the most growth you can experience as an individual often comes from the deepest wounds you will experience in your life. These deep wounds create a unique opportunity for us. They invite us to become a more embodied version of our truest self—the self we were born to be. These wounds are more valuable than any achievement or accolade.

17

Although I only had my dad for a short 16 years, one of the most powerful lessons he taught me was to be a life-long learner. I have used this mindset to launch an investigation into the great potential of what we can become when we choose to rise with the heat of the fire of loss rather than smolder in the ashes. This investigation started in a short ten-minute Ignite talk I gave in 2014.

In my opening line, I called Elisabeth Kübler-Ross' Five Stages of Grief a load of crap. Ironically, that was probably the anger talking. It was also because, having been through grief twice, I had found these Five Stages to be far too limiting to fully encompass the range of emotions I felt. I found myself wondering how to go deeper into exploring what else we can do to support those who struggle after the loss of a loved one so that we are living a full life in the aftermath of such an event.

Because really, it isn't about just getting through the stages of grief. It's about truly living while grief still exists in us. It's about experiencing purpose and growth from our grief. That was the beginning of developing what would later be my five elements.

So, after we've exhausted the traditional Five Stages of Grief and arrived at Acceptance—even if we're in the darkest, coldest, loneliest emotional place imaginable—we must open ourselves to doing the work that will support a lifetime of grief. Acceptance does not guarantee happiness. Acceptance is not the end of grief. It is really just a beginning—of taking action.

As I continued to reflect on Kübler-Ross' commonly accepted model for grief, I could see the need for an explanation of what to expect from someone grieving. I ruminated over the traditional stages of grief, wondering what it was about them that I didn't like and why I had felt there had to be a better way. I realized that I wanted something that was more proactive and helped me learn from and live with my loss. I needed elements of action to guide me.

Part of what I learned in my investigation of Kübler-Ross' original work was that her initial goal was to improve the medical community's ability to treat and support terminal patients. This model was created to work best when applied to those on the outside looking in to help and understand a person grieving their own mortality.

It started to make more sense. These Five Stages were not designed or intended to provide a map for the person experiencing the loss! This explains why people healing from the loss of a loved one are left with the feeling of "now what?" or "is this all there is?" Grieving people are still not able to fully integrate the experience of loss and go on to live a full life.

In essence, the Five Stages just describe what we initially go through. They are a jumping off point for taking action.

PRAISE FOR ELISABETH KÜBLER–ROSS' FIVE STAGES OF GRIEF

Elisabeth Kübler-Ross was an incredible and compassionate Swiss-American psychiatrist who developed the Five Stages of Grief as we know them today. Since Kübler-Ross' theory was published in the late 1960s, it has come under both criticism and

19

acclaim. She, herself, acknowledged that her explanation was not designed to be a linear progression. She stated later in her career that she regretted it had been somewhat misconstrued in the application. The foremost misunderstanding is the application of these Five Stages to that of grieving the loss of a loved one. Kübler-Ross' work and research was in fact meant to help the terminally ill accept the reality of their own impending death.

Most importantly, Kübler-Ross' Five Stages of Grief began a conversation about grief and loss that, up until that point, no one had braved. That in and of itself should be celebrated. I am glad she did it. In order to face grief, we have to start the conversation. I believe the cultural shift she created by introducing this conversation and encouraging people to acknowledge grief and loss as an integral part of our humanness is no less important than the women's rights movement of the 1970s.

Kübler-Ross unveiled her work on the Five Stages of Grief in her 1969 book, *On Death and Dying*.[3] In the time since it was published, her concepts have become the commonly accepted theory on grieving by the general public.

The Five Stages, as developed by Kübler-Ross, are described below, including a brief description of each:

1. **Denial** — "There's been a mistake, this isn't really happening to me." "Let's get a second opinion."

2. **Anger** —"This isn't fair." "Who did this?" "Someone is going to pay for this!" "He/She is wrong!"

3. **Bargaining** — "If I get cured I'll never smoke again." This, the third stage, is especially prevalent in cases where death may be imminent.

4. **Depression** — "Life is not worth living." "Nothing is going to get better." "I miss my loved one, why go on?"

5. **Acceptance** — "What's done is done." "My loved one is not coming back." "I am at peace with the time I have left."

While I did go through these stages somewhat when I lost my father and again when I lost my son, it didn't explain everything. They just explained stages. But there was more to it than that. I felt like the more I dug into the traditional Five Stages of Grief, the more I didn't know how to re-create a life I loved, much less thrive after losing my son. What I really needed were elements of action. What was I to do?

Then, when I reflected on the lessons I learned from Daniel's experience and my own mindfulness as a yoga teacher, it began to become clear what I needed to do for myself, and later what I would teach others. I began to outline a system that would support me as I created a meaningful life, lived in alignment with my true self, and honored the memory of my son, Brandon.

During Daniel's treatment in the years before Brandon's death, there were many twists and unexpected turns. During one of those twists I was told by one of the people who was an integral part of my team, "Looks like you have another AFGO!" I looked at him with total confusion. With a smirk on his face, he followed up with, "You know—Another F***ing Growth Opportunity!" I certainly knew what those were. The truth was, at that point I was really over AFGOs! Hadn't I already had my share? Still, his words stuck with me. I began a habit of regularly flipping my problems, both personal and professional, into AFGOs.

It changed my mindset and would allow me to focus on a solution and *growth opportunity* rather than the problem. So many times, when we grieve we only focus on the sadness and the loss. While not easy, focusing on growth is key. This mindset served me after Brandon's death and although there was so much more to learn, I had a strong foundation of growth through emotional pain and my dad's wisdom to be a lifelong learner.

I realized that the framework from the Five Stages of Grief is too limiting. The stages wouldn't provide me the AFGOs I needed. I could certainly find Acceptance of Brandon's death and notice when Anger or Denial were rearing their heads. But another thing I said in that talk in 2014 was that acceptance is another word for "resignation"—and what I couldn't accept was a life of resignation!

In all this, I've come to believe that we need both the traditional Five Stages, plus the system I have constructed for genuine healing of the total person. And both are of great value when the desired outcome is to fully integrate all our life's experiences. I call them the **Five Elements of Action**.

FIVE ELEMENTS OF ACTION

Healing fully requires that we believe in our own inner wisdom to heal. It also requires that we invest our energy into behaviors and shifts in our mindset that will create the greatest return on our investment. Grief is not one size fits all, and it's not a nice tidy process of events that passively wash over us.

Healing from a traumatic loss requires that we not just react, but commit to taking action. We have to be willing to get our hands dirty and be brave enough to do the work even when doing the work creates more—though usually temporary—pain than staying where we are. We have to do this because the result of this work takes us in the direction of becoming whole in the nature of our true self.

In this book, I've outlined **Five Elements of Action**. They are behaviors and mindset shifts I've developed over years of dealing with my own grief and helping others face theirs. I call it my Crazy Good Grief work. Beyond that, I blog, speak, consult, and offer retreats to try to help as many people as I can. I have been amazed at the results I have seen and the feedback I've gotten.

The design of these elements is interchangeable and elastic, and can be moved between and around as your grief changes—and it will, I promise. These elements also provide the framework to deepen your relationships with others. By doing this work, you will create a more intimate connection to your true self.

This book will help you achieve a healing and growth mindset. When you do this work, you become more resilient and able to bounce back from all that life throws your way. I chose not to number them because there is not an order in which you must work through them, and they are all connected and interchangeable. Here are **the Five Elements of Action** covered in this book.

- **Wellness and Self-care:** This becomes one of the most important and powerful tools for managing grief and avoiding other losses that threaten our quality of life.

- **Letting Go of Limiting Beliefs:** Working through thought patterns that keep us stuck and unable to move forward.

- **Loving Self and Others:** How to release the guilt and shame that keeps us feeling unworthy, which also limits our ability to have deep, meaningful connections with others.

- **Creating Connections that Heal:** The essential layering of connecting to our own inner wisdom, cultivating new communities that understand our loss, and positively engaging with family and friends.

- **Gratitude:** If reclaiming happiness in our life after loss is the goal, then learning to cultivate gratitude becomes the bridge from sadness to joy.

HOW TO USE THIS BOOK

My hope for you is that you can use this book for many, many years to come. The essence of this book addresses the mind, body, and spirit and shares what I like to call "elements in action." You can't just sit and let grief take over. Time alone isn't enough to heal you. The old adage, "Time heals all wounds," couldn't be further from the truth. Time may dull the pain, but it doesn't give purpose to the hurt and pain you've felt. It doesn't help you grow.

Grief is a lifelong process. The goal should be to positively integrate both good and bad experiences. To do that, we must be willing to do the work that matters most.

This book shares each of the elements of action and why they are integral parts of healing. At the end of each chapter, you will find suggestions on how to integrate that element into your personal life. That will be your "elements in action."

I have developed these elements over many painful years of grieving. All five have played a valuable role in my own healing journey. I continue to move between these concepts, depending on what is happening with my grief and life.

As I approached the five-year anniversary of Brandon's death, I reflected on what behaviors had made the biggest shifts in my ability to integrate this experience into my life. In doing so, I also brought to light mistakes I'd made and places where I was way off course. Honestly reflecting on the things I'd done wrong was more helpful than what I'd done right!

These elements are organized so that they all grow and expand with your healing process. As a result, you can use this book beyond the early raw grief you may be feeling now.

As you begin this positive, uplifting part of your healing journey, feel free to jump into any of the five elements. Explore the concepts in each chapter and do the work in that section.

I recommend keeping a journal close by when you read the chapter where you can do the work at the end, write down ideas that come to mind or questions you have that you want to ruminate on, and ask the most healed version of yourself to answer.

I hold a deep belief that each of us possess the knowledge and wisdom we need to heal ourselves. Learning to listen to our own inner wisdom is one of the best ways to reveal the knowledge about what heals us.

Here we go. Let's start this healing journey.

1

PERSONIFY YOUR GRIEF

The Guest House
By Rumi

This being human is a guest house
Every morning a new arrival.
A joy, a depression, a meanness,
some momentary awareness comes
as an unexpected visitor.
Welcome and entertain them all!
Even if they are a crowd of sorrows,
who violently sweep your house
empty of its furniture,
still treat each guest honorably.
He may be clearing you out for some new delight.
The dark thought, the shame, the malice,
meet them at the door laughing,
and invite them in.
Be grateful for whoever comes,
because each has been sent
as a guide from beyond.[4]

I read this poem long before the grief of child loss violently swept my house of everything I knew to be true. Back then, it felt like a wonderful and gentle reminder to allow all of our feelings in the simple day-to-day struggles of life. It would take Brandon's death for me to see the deeper meaning of these words. Then, when I read this poem again, I struggled with this idea—the idea of embracing all that I felt. Of *welcoming* and *entertaining* grief! Of thinking it could create some "new delight." The last thing I could possibly fathom was that perhaps there was even a hidden opportunity.

The part of that poem that I find especially enlightening is the line, "treat each guest honorably." Grief was my new guest that I didn't want but had to figure out what to do with. Prior to losing Brandon, if someone had asked me if grief is "honorable," I would have told them, "No way!" Tell grief to get the hell out! But just try telling grief to leave.

What would you say if someone asked you if grief was "honorable"? Is grief, with its predisposition to anger, depression, and resentment, worthy of honor?

We live in a culture that believes in the pursuit of happiness, and grief is the antithesis of this pursuit. Grief feels like playing a game of Monopoly and being told not to pass go and not to collect $200. Grief feels like you're being punished for something.

In my early, raw grief, I embraced my punishment. As you will read later in this book, I punished myself. Rather than viewing grief as honorable or sacred, I felt condemned and unworthy. It was through the consistent practice of the elements contained in this book that I was able to shift my insight about the gifts grief was bestowing on me. Now I can say without reservation that I am deeply grateful for the awakening journey grief has taken me on.

The journey and use of the elements I share in this book have been the sandpaper that's revealed a deeper, more meaningful life and purpose. When we embrace this, it entices us to do the hard work that will lead us to reveal the person we were always meant to become. The highest version of ourselves.

The truth is, of all the emotions we feel as humans, grief is most worthy of honor and respect. So before we get into the elements of action, let's understand grief and how we need to treat it.

HONORING GRIEF (AND YOURSELF)

When I think of honoring my grief, I imagine myself as the person who picks up my trash—my grief—every week. No one wants that job; it's smelly and it's full of all the unusable, discarded things other people don't want. Quite possibly it's full of other people's avoidance of grief...beer and wine bottles, wrappers from emotional eating benders, etc. Or, perhaps I'm just sharing with you what was in my garbage in the early months of my grief. Yes, alcohol and I became BFFs for a period of time, and I could eat an entire batch of cookies before my husband knew they had even been baked! I'm sure he wondered why the house smelled of fresh-baked cookies, but there were never any cookies.

But despite the hard and dirty parts of the job, the garbage carrier (i.e. the grief carrier, *YOU*) is honorable. And yes, the trash or grief itself is honorable. Just like the poem says, he's "clearing the way for some new delight." Without honoring our grief and giving it a purpose, our emotional garbage is going to start to pile up and get real stinky for us and those around us. This is not easy at first. For a while you want to just let it pile up, and you don't really care who can smell it.

At some point, however, it gets unbearable. You become buried in it. So then the questions become, how do you deal with grief? What can you do with it? What do you say to this unwelcome and yet honorable guest? It has taken me years to realize the answer, and it seems to be counterintuitive.

You need to cultivate a loving relationship with your grief. It's here to teach you the most important lessons you may ever learn.

The longer I live with grief as my constant companion, the more I get curious about what it needs to thrive, and as such allows me to thrive. I have found that, just like you and me, grief does best when it has a purpose or a reason for existing. It's human nature to want to feel needed. And as grief is a part of the human experience, it would make sense then that we need to personify it and give it a purpose.

However, there is a disconnect. To see grief as needing a job and needing purpose, we need to understand the value and healing that occurs when we treat it honorably. One of the reasons we struggle with grief is this:

We're never taught what to do with it.

A trash person knows where to take the trash. But as grievers, is there a place to put our grief? Not really. So what do we do with it? It sits there on the curb, with us standing there begging for help. Subsequently, it becomes uncomfortable in our own lives and in the lives of those trying to support us.

YOU VS. YOUR GRIEF

You are more than your grief. You always have been and you always will be. Grief is a separate entity from you. This is a truth that doesn't feel real in the early stages. In early, raw grief, it feels as if grief is consuming us, and everything we were before is now infected with this unwanted virus of grief.

I will be the first one to say that grief has the potential to completely change everything about us—for good and bad. It changes things like how we identify as parents, siblings, or spouses. It can alter our spiritual beliefs and even cause us to do things that we never thought we'd do. But what we don't realize is that we have much more control over how grief changes us than we may think. As a matter of fact, we have 100% control over how we integrate grief and our loss into our lives.

Below is a variation on what is known as Parts Work. Parts Work is an aspect of the Internal Family Systems (IFS) model created in the 1980s by Richard Schwartz.[5] In the way I present it here, it's a way of understanding how grief becomes a part of us and why. It also explains why I believe we can regulate the effects it has on our lives.

31

Imagine this scenario with me...

You are the chairman of the board for a very important company. As the chairman of this most epic company, you've invited your board members to a meeting. You look around the conference table and you see each of the following people:

A Mom, an Entrepreneur, a Professor, a Yogi, a Runner, a Creative Writer, a Chubby Girl, a Woman Who Lost Her Son a few years ago, and a few other members. Each board member has a seat at the table, and you as the chairman sit at the head. Just as you are about to begin the meeting, in comes a board member known to be a loud, angry, raucous drunk who ruins every event she attends. You roll your eyes, but let her take her seat.

Grief has arrived.

The very important company you are the chairman of is *your life,* and the board members represent the many parts of who you are. In this example, I've actually used my own board members. They represent some of the many parts of me that make up the person the world sees on any given day in a particular situation. You too are made up of parts that create the total person you are.

What are all the parts of who you are?

At the head of these parts, the chairman is the pure, beautiful and total essence of who you are. This is what I call your soul or life force. This chairman could also be called your inner wisdom. It is the part of you that directs what you were born to become. When your life is moving in flow and synchronicity on a day-today basis, your inner wisdom is able to guide you. Unfortunately, sometimes we allow other parts of ourselves to take over and run things. This especially happens when Grief enters the room unwelcome. Grief is not your inner wisdom; it is a part of you that has recently arrived at the board meeting. It is, however, a part of your life you never really wanted and would never have invited. You also have parts of you that:

1. You were born with (personal characteristics) and,

2. You have incorporated along the way as a result of your environment.

All of our parts are created to keep us safe, happy, or simply alive, but they all have our best intentions at heart. For example, in my case, I was certainly born a Runner. I have always been very kinesthetic and movement based, but the part of me that has run marathons only arrived on the scene in my early thirties. With the loss of my father, and subsequent losses, I've used running as a coping mechanism for my grief. I would also like to add here that another running related part of me is the coping mechanism of running away from my problems. Out of necessity, my Runner part has become very busy!

Using the IFS theory, the parts that surround your soul are what make up your human experience in this world. They are needed to manifest your unique purpose for being here and what your soul's deepest desires are. In addition to your soul and different parts, there is also a connection to Spirit. Using titles such as God, Allah, Shiva or Buddha, Spirit could be defined by your religious upbringing, or simply as a feeling of connection to a force greater than yourself; perhaps you call it the Divine or

Spirit. Whatever Spirit is for you, it's a recognition that your soul is an agent of this greater power and that each of us has a divine and unique purpose.

Back to the board meeting...

When Grief shows up, it can't help itself. It has a pretty explosive personality. It takes over the meeting. It doesn't let the other parts weigh in on decisions, and it certainly tries to keep your inner wisdom from having any say as to how this meeting might be an opportunity to deepen into its unique purpose. No, Grief becomes the *only* voice at the meeting.

Ah, but remember I said that all our parts want what's best for us and want to act in a way that elevates our life's purpose? So what does that mean when we give Grief a seat at the table? What do we do with Grief? What is its purpose?

The purpose of Grief is to give us a vehicle that allows us to process and integrate the experience of losing a loved one and use our suffering to become a better version of ourselves.

Let me put this another way. Within all our parts, there are always some that seem difficult to deal with or that get out of hand and tip the balance of our lives. For example, a person who has a part of themselves that is an Addict. That part was created, possibly, to avoid social awkwardness. Remember, all parts want what is good for us, though "good" is relative. But then when a part becomes too much and takes over, bad things happen. The Addict part of that person might want to fill the bathtub with bourbon and get a straw! Other parts and even the inner wisdom knows this isn't good, but this Addict part is out of control.

Grief has that same potential, especially if we just let it do what it wants. It will run completely out of control if we don't get to know it and give it a purpose.

Grief deserves a place on the board of directors, but it doesn't deserve to come in and take over the entire company! It takes a bit of practice to get Grief to sit down and behave. Grief can also be sneaky to get its way and sometimes you will notice that your Grief will partner up with other parts of you. These aren't usually good collaborations. The example of the Addict is that it is also a great partner for Grief. The Addict wants to numb the pain and Grief has pain to be numbed! These two parts see it as a win-win for your well-being, even though it leads to disaster.

Ultimately, you need to stick up for yourself and figure out how to follow your inner wisdom. You are still the chairman of the board and need to make decisions based on the input from your board members. In Chapter 5 we will dig deeper into how to connect and listen to your inner wisdom. This can be an incredibly daunting task when you are grieving, which is why we must get to know our grief and give it purpose.

Cultivating a Relationship with Grief

Grief is very strongly associated with love. It's as if grief and love are the two sides of the same coin, if you will. There is one side that represents the love you have for someone, and the other side is the loss you feel when they are gone. Love and grief are closely woven and knit together. That's why when you love someone so much, it hurts so much to lose them.

The more love we have for a person, the deeper the loss feels.

It's also like a great pendulum swing—the stronger the love, the stronger the pendulum swings to the other side, which is grief. It is not the absence of love as much as it is the deeply felt presence of it that causes the swing in the face of loss.

I'm not suggesting that you stay in the raw, deep grief simply because the love is also still there. I am sharing a way for you to cultivate a relationship with your grief that grows, changes, and matures just as any loving relationship does. To do this, we must give it time, attention, and room to grow.

In many ways, grief is like a person. But just like a person, it starts out one way and develops as it goes along. If you've ever had a baby, you know that to care for a newborn is draining. You have to feed it every couple of hours, and in the process of caring for it, you don't get enough sleep; it takes all of your energy, and it is exhausting! Slowly as the infant grows, you can go longer without having to feed it, you begin to get a little more sleep, and you eventually feel less exhausted.

The early feelings of grief are very much the same. Every few minutes, we feel grief asking for our attention; it keeps us up at night and we can't do anything without it being connected to us 24/7. And just like with a newborn—friends and family come by and offer support, sometimes by way of frozen casseroles— but the truth is that the actual rearing of grief is on us.

Throughout the first year after Brandon died, when a holiday or event would come up, people were quick to recognize the importance of all the "firsts." Just like when a baby is born and we celebrate their firsts—first smile, first tooth, first step, and so on until we get to the ever important first birthday. It comes naturally for our culture to focus on the firsts, even with loss. Oddly, of the holidays that first year, Valentine's Day was the worst one for me. It was painful to be so aware that Brandon would never come home with that warm twinkle in his chocolate brown eyes and his Kool-aid smile and say he had met "the one."

Knowing I would never be at his wedding or watch him hold a new baby who would be his pride and joy was tough. Similar to accepting there would be no one to walk me down the aisle at my wedding or be a grandfather to my children when my father died. Loss forced us to erase so many anticipated firsts.

Like a baby, grief outgrows the firsts and becomes somewhat of a toddler. It starts to get a mind of its own. Many people express that the second year after loss is harder. They have more angst and resentment, and they feel more abandoned by friends and family, who they might resent for "moving on" or "forgetting" our loss. In other words, by year two, your grief has reached the terrible twos. By the time we have a toddler in the house, we realize that it's important to give grief purpose. More importantly, to give it a purpose that meets that toddler with appropriate skills, abilities and knowledge. Grief, it seems, is growing up.

The longer we engage this lifelong relationship with grief, the more we develop an intimate relationship with it. One of the most powerful things we can do with our grief is be open and welcoming to it changing over time.

Your grief for what you've lost also needs a purpose that is appropriate to its stage of development. For example, when your grief is new (like a newborn), you need to nurture it. Pay attention to it while you also surround yourself with love and compassion. As it grows, you can start to let go a bit, but you still need to give it enough nurturing to thrive.

But, remember to treat it as it needs to be treated, *when* it needs to be treated. If you were to treat your teenager the same way you did a newborn, things wouldn't go so well because their needs are very different.

The one thing they both have in common is that they both need support, direction, and purpose. Once you've navigated the initial stages of grief, the time will come to employ a different type of support for your relationship with grief.

Early in my grief I journaled a lot, and on the four-month anniversary of Brandon's death I wrote:

> *Tomorrow is four months. Writing that makes me think of how, when a baby is born, we count their lives in months, often for the first 2-3 years. I guess grief is like a small child – you count it in small increments. If I could I would count it in days. I feel like it will take a lifetime for 'grief' to outgrow me, or just like a child we begin to simply mark the years...unless your child dies. Then you start over counting the days, weeks,*

months all over again. I was up to 21 years, 4 months, 27 days. Now I'm back to 121 days and counting my life sentence.

Now, years later, I no longer feel the acute constant pain I did in those raw, early months nor do I still feel like it's a life sentence. Occasionally I will still compare the time with Brandon to the time without. I still have my relationship with him and my cherished memories, but now I have this new relationship with grief to cultivate and learn about. A relationship with grief is a *part* of my relationship with Brandon, not in place of it. Brandon's death has taught me so much, just as his life did. My relationship with Brandon continues to change, just like my grief does.

GRIEF HAS NO DEADLINE

An essential break down in how we've been taught to grieve is the culturally accepted idea that we have 365 days to grieve, and then we should be ready to move on. I'm not sure why this is, but somehow people who aren't grieving tell those who are grieving that 365 days is "enough." Somehow, magically, we should be done on day 366. I've talked with so many people who express deep sadness over friends and family who, after the first year is over, encourage them to move on when they clearly can never do so.

Let's apply the same mindset of a year to get over grief to that of a loving marriage. Imagine if you got married on May 12th this year, and so on May 13th of next year, society suggests that you've been loving enough! Now it's time to move on. How would that make you feel?

39

What if instead of celebrating your love continuing on for years and years, people became disgusted? What if when you talked about the love you feel for your beloved, people give you that look? Or they gently remind you, "Quit living in the past; it's time to move on!" What would happen if you accepted this advice and you began not acting with love toward your spouse? You then quit making time for him/her, were impatient when he/she had a bad day, ignored him/her when they wanted to spend time together, etc. Well, being once divorced, I can tell you how that works out.

Stopping loving someone doesn't make sense when they are alive, and it certainly doesn't make sense even if they have died.

I hope that helps you and others understand that if we are to understand grief over the loss of a loved one as the result of deep love, then we can no more put a timeline on it than we can for love of a living person. It's ironic that we expect love to last "until death do we part," but when we part with a loved one in death it becomes "until 365 days do we grieve." The reality is, grief knows no deadline, because love knows no bounds.

LOVE IN ACTION VS. GRIEF IN ACTION

In the dictionary, under the definition of "love" you will see it listed as both a noun and a verb, but "grief" is only defined as a noun. The word "grieving" is a verb to describe the result of a loss, and we need to begin thinking of grief as a word meaning to take action.

In our human experience, we usually learn about love at an early age and are able to act on it and put it into practice by mimicking what we see others do. We learn that when we care for someone, we are taking action. We do kind things, we buy necessary items or gifts, we make pleasant conversation and give words of encouragement. We learn that love is visible in our actions. To love someone is to take action to manifest and create what that love looks like and how we want it to show up in our life.

Naturally, there are many different types of love, and how we express these will differ based on our individual circumstance.

Grief, on the other hand, is not so easily learned. We don't have as many opportunities to practice this emotion, which is a good thing. When we do have opportunities to observe it and learn about it, honestly, our culture is horrible at it. Quite frankly, we don't learn much because what we observe is usually acting out in ways we don't quite understand. In addition, it's not a pleasant thing to talk about or experience. So, we want to protect ourselves from experiencing and navigating grief, because the pain of grief can be overwhelming.

What we do learn from watching the negative parts of grief is that people don't want to let it run willy-nilly all over the place like we allow love to do. We want grief to be tightly controlled and put on a short leash. We want to make it something we can fix or cure in a set period of time—365 days to be precise (and that's when it's an "important" loss).

We are not raised in cultures or by people who "grieve well." I remember wishing for a way to convey to others what I was feeling but without saying anything. I wished I could just wear black all the time to signal to the outside world I was in "mourning." There were many days I would've liked to have hung a little sign around my neck that read:

"I'm grieving the loss of my son. My heart feels heavy and just leaving my house today was really hard. Oh, and I'm sorry for anything I say or do that is mean or hateful, it's the grief talking."

The people at my local Starbucks would've benefitted from this warning as I came in the door. Those chipper baristas were in my crosshairs more than once as I stopped by on my way to work. I'm surprised the manager didn't issue flak jackets during the hours I might show up. But, if I could've worn my sign, they would've quit asking me how my day was going or what fun plans I had for the weekend. The problem was, they wouldn't have known what to say that could help me—because we aren't taught what to say.

I get it. Grief is just plain hard. But after having to go through it, I can tell you that grief has something to teach us if we will listen. At its core, grief must be felt and experienced on an individual level for us to genuinely appreciate the magnitude of this emotion. Clearly, we have some work to do as individuals and as a society to better understand and work through grief.

THE LANGUAGE OF GRIEF

The book *The Five Love Languages: How to Express Heartfelt Commitment to Your Mate* by Gary Chapman[6] is a great outline for how we can overlay the concept of turning grief into an action as well. In his book, Chapman explains that each of us has a distinct way in which we feel loved. He put these into the five categories of:

1. Words of affirmation

2. Acts of service

3. Receiving gifts

4. Physical touch

5. Quality time

Chapman flips the old adage, "Treat people the way YOU want to be treated" to "Treat people the way THEY want to be treated." He explains that each of us feel love in a different way, and typically we have a couple ways we feel loved by those around us.

Take my husband, Scott, and me. We are the definition of opposites attract, and that includes our love languages. My wonderful husband feels most loved with "acts of service." When I do things like clean the kitchen and go out of my way to get things done around the house, he feels loved and appreciated. Well, let me tell you a thing or two.... I am horrible at cleaning house and doing chores, and it's not in my wheelhouse as a way to express love. Which is why he's my hunky housekeeper!

43

PAULA STEPHENS, MA

My primary love language, on the other hand, is "quality time." Spend time with me, turn off ESPN, quit cleaning the house, and let's go do something together. When I can have him all to myself and we can connect, it fills my love tank!

My secondary love language is "words of affirmation." Unfortunately for me, Scott is a quiet introvert who was not raised on words of affirmation. It never occurs to him to use words to express his love. However, I have learned that when I come home and he's cleaned the house or picked up dog poop out of the back yard, he is "saying" how much he loves me.

I have also learned that, as much as I don't like cleaning house, with a little effort on my part, he feels loved and knows I care for him. His secondary love language is "physical touch." I've learned that snuggling up next to him to watch a football game goes a long way to filling his love tank.

When we put our love into the right action, it is so much more effective and has a greater impact. Now, I know what you're thinking. This is a book about grief, why am I explaining the love languages?

If we are to accept grief as the pendulum swing of love AND we accept that love is an action specific to an individual need, then we must manifest action for our grief. More specifically, the *correct* action for our grief.

GRIEVING AND OUR CULTURE

Culturally, the best we've ever been able to do with applying the concept of action for grief is Kübler-Ross' Five Stages of Grief.

1. Denial

2. Bargaining

3. Anger

4. Depression

5. Acceptance

The main difference between the Love Languages and the Stages of Grief is that the Love Languages allow us to meet love where it is. This allows us to know how to take the best action with adoration being the desired outcome. In a marriage, we have already taken time to get to know each other, and over time, we realize what love means to the other person. With grief, we lack a guidance system to meet it where it is. We need to learn about it, get curious about it, and then take action with HEALING being the desired outcome.

As you will see in the following chapters, each of the Five Elements of Action gives us *specific action* to meet our grief where it is. Grief should be approached in the same way we cultivate a relationship with another human being. We go into it knowing nothing about it, what makes it feel good and cared for or what enrages it and makes it angry. But over time, we take the time and energy to get to know those answers, and then respond accordingly.

Give Grief a Purpose

Giving grief a purpose means to give it attention and a place/ time to express itself. This means to do things to remember your loved one, no matter what anyone else thinks. For example, plan to celebrate your loved one's birthday in some way—have a quiet moment at the beach or take a walk in nature and have a conversation with them. Give your grief the energy when it needs it—give it your attention. When you do, the Starbucks baristas might not have as much to worry about that day or week. Your grief is occupied for a time and it won't come screaming up to the poor 20-something barista about being out of non-fat milk.

When we work to develop healthy relationships with other people, we begin to know what's going on with them. We need to take a similar approach with our grief. When we take the time to nurture this new relationship, get to know it and its quirks, then we can take appropriate action.

For example, have you ever taken a tired toddler grocery shopping? Not a good combination for anyone. There is screaming and crying and confusion. Early in my grief, grocery shopping was hard for me; it was exhausting. One time I remember being so proud of myself. I left work and went to the store to buy stuff for dinner—probably a first in months! In my mind, I bought everything I needed for tortellini soup. It took everything I had to make it through the store without having a meltdown (damn cheery checkout people). When I got home, what I had was the most random concoction of ingredients. No matter how you put them together, it wasn't going to make soup. I bawled.

Maybe in reading that you thought, "That's normal. Life is just hard when you have grief." Yes, that's true, but doing daily tasks can be easier if we give grief the attention it needs first. If you had a toddler, you'd let him have a nap first, or you'd give him a hug and talk to him, or you'd help him feel safe and that shopping would be ok.

Same thing with grief. If I had left work, sat in my car for a moment and checked in with my grief, I would've realized I was taking a toddler to the grocery store. I would have reflected on how emotional the day had been and how temperamental my grief was being. I would have acknowledged the state of my grief. Just giving this little bit of attention to grief is all it really needs.

Well hello, Grief! Here you are again. I see you.

Had I done this, I probably would've done one of two things: Gone straight home, or if we really needed soup for dinner, I would have run in and bought a damn can of Campbell's! Remember, we're trying to cultivate a healthy relationship with grief and give it a job so we can function better in other ways. There will be some compromise. If that means a can of soup instead of homemade, then so be it. What I didn't realize at the time was that my grief was still young; it needed peace and quiet and a place to rest its head.

Using the example above, here are several ways I could've given my grief a job so I could go on with other things:

- Take time to journal about the day.

- Go for a walk.

- Create a tradition to remember your loved one's birthday and/or the anniversary of their death.

- Spend time alone with your grief.

- Spend time volunteering at a place that reminds you of your loved one.

These are great ways to give attention to your grief and give it purpose. But then there are moments when grief needs your immediate attention. A song on the radio, a smell, or a memory hits hard. In these moments, create the habit of tending to your grief with deep breaths and breathe into the immense power of those moments. Recognizing this as grief speaking up. Give it a moment, acknowledge it, and move forward.

Here are some affirmations you can repeat to yourself while sitting in your car, or run them through your head:

- I miss my loved one. I will always love him/her.

- My grief is strong, but it is not in charge of who I am.

- I will give my grief purpose.

- I am more than my grief. I always have been and I always will be.

- My grief is a reminder of the love I continue to feel for my loved one.

As you go through this book, each of the Five Elements of Action are designed to keep your grief healthy and not take over the board meeting. You will learn to use these elements to deepen the connection to your inner wisdom. This will begin to give purpose to our life's experience so that you can blend your grief into the total person that you are.

Treat grief honorably. As the Rumi poem suggests, "even if they're a crowd of sorrows, who violently sweep your house empty of its furniture, still, treat each guest honorably."[7] Allow it to have a voice, but also make sure that it's being given the *correct* type of direction from you so that it becomes a beautiful part of who you are.

The following chapters are written so you are able to give grief exactly what it needs. As you become more courageous and brave in your exploration of your grief, you will notice it changing. As it changes, you will be able to get back to old things you love, try new things, and begin living again.

By reading this book, you have committed to grieving better. It is my hope that by doing this, you will become the new generation of what grief *should* look like. You will put an end to our only cultural grief tradition—the presentation of your finest freezable casserole. Your actions will show how empowering grief can be when we lean into it, get curious about it, and explore it like an ancient warrior exploring a new frontier.

ELEMENT IN ACTION:

- Visualize your grief. Does it have a color, smell, texture, or weight to it? Write it down.

- Are there "parts" of you that your grief partners with to throw your life off course even more?

- Which part of you has the loudest voice in the boardroom?

- Think about your grief as it is right now in your life. How old would you describe it as being? Not in relationship to your time since your loss, but how does it behave?

2

ELEMENT: WELLNESS AND SELF-CARE

"The body is the temple of the soul, the temple of your spirit. The vehicle for you to become one with God. Honor it. Take care of it."

—Ram Dass,
Polishing the Mirror[8]

If you're like most people, when you hear words like fitness, wellness, or self-care, you probably start to envision different types of exercise or maybe you think of the latest diet fad. I imagine that if you are reading this after losing a loved one, this topic might make you feel completely overwhelmed. After all, you might not have the energy to get out of bed, much less go to the gym.

I have good news for you. In this chapter when I talk about your wellness and self-care, it's about meeting you where you are *today* with the energy you have *today*.

My entire professional career has been the study of human performance and wellness. My formal education is a Master's degree in exercise physiology with certifications as a Wellness Coach and Yoga Instructor. Spanning my 25-year career, I've also worked in fitness and wellness management and been a group fitness instructor and personal trainer. Some of my most enjoyable work came when I worked in cardiac rehab, not just because that's where I met my husband, but because working with people who had experienced such life changing events was truly gratifying; I have similar feelings about the work I do now with healing loss.

My dad was a college professor and one thing I certainly got from him was an innate desire to teach. In the most recent years of my professional career, I've worked as a national presenter for the American College of Sports Medicine and an adjunct professor at Metro State University in Denver in the Human Performance and Sport department. My love of teaching and sharing knowledge is what led me to write this book.

I share this to let you know that wellness is a passion of mine, but also to acknowledge that even with all the education and experience I had under my belt, grief was still more powerful. That is, until I began to apply the concepts of parts work from Chapter 1 and I created my board of directors and became committed to having a positive relationship with my grief.

It's important that we put the concept of wellness and self-care into a context with which you can identify. Culturally, we often identify wellness or self-care as behaviors we temporarily change—such as dieting or working out—that result in changes to our appearance. For example, we change the food we eat based on a current fad diet in hopes of losing weight, or we start an exercise program to tone up the saggy spots. Those are all fine things.

But in the context of grief, I want something more for you. I want you to think about your *entire* self—all the parts that make you who you are—and begin to act in a compassionate and healing way toward all the aspects that create wellness for you. First, I want to explain the three dimensions that encompass your soul or life force, and then we can go into the five areas that cover your different states of wellness.

BODY AND SPIRIT

Your body is the physical manifestation of Spirit. How we love and treat our bodies must be in alignment with the care and treatment we give our mental and emotional state. With my background in wellness, one of the biggest disconnects I've seen in the grief paradigm is a lack of attention to how powerful the use, or misuse, of our bodies is in the healing process. I consider it equivalent to someone needing a wheelchair and not being provided mental health support to understand the psychological issues of such a dramatic change in the physical body.

Honor and take care of your body, just as you do your emotional healing. The mind and the body are made of energy, and the physical body is the most accessible way to manipulate and balance your emotional energy.

YOUR THREE-LEGGED SOUL TABLE

I invite you to understand wellness by sharing an exercise I do with the participants of the healing retreats I offer. At these retreats, I work with people who've lost a loved one and bring them together in a beautiful nature setting where we can focus on our healing and feel supported by those who understand what we're going through. We practice yoga, meditation and share personal reflections. Hosting these retreats in beautiful locations such as the Rocky Mountains or Costa Rica encourages us to notice the perfect flow of nature and align ourselves with this energy. But you can certainly also reach healing at your own pace and in your own place.

Let's start the exercise. Close your eyes. Imagine a three-legged table. Each leg of the table represents the following three dimensions:

- Your mind

- Your body

- Your heart

On the table sits your soul, or however you feel comfortable referring to the essence of your being. Now think about those three legs. Are they balanced? Which one seems to be holding up well, and which one is not?

In order for us to operate at the highest level possible, use our unique talents and abilities, and heal our hurts, we need to feel balanced and whole in all three dimensions. When one of these is out of balance, not only does it create a discrepancy with how we feel at our core, it causes the other two to work harder to compensate. After a while, the table will inevitably fall over.

Wellness is an integration of ALL the parts of us that support our deepest desire to live a full life. We can't pay attention to one or two without finding a way to check in and find balance between all three.

Developing your wellness and self-care are so important and will impact other elements discussed in later chapters. The ability to develop habits that support self-care will be directly supported by doing the work to love yourself in Chapter 4, as well as the importance of cultivating a mindset of gratitude in Chapter 6. You will also see when we talk about connections, in Chapter 5, how self-care supports the connections that heal us. All of the work in this book is designed to balance your mind, body, and heart and we start with wellness.

The first thing you must do is care for yourself enough so that your three-legged soul table can balance on its own. How can you do this?

- Get enough rest.

- Eat wholesome meals.

- Talk to a trusted friend or counselor.

- Allow yourself to grieve.

Especially at the onset of grief, you may find it hard to just take care of your own basic needs: getting up in the morning, taking a shower, breathing. That's why we start here. Wellness and self-care must begin on a basic level. Once the basic things get easier, you can then move on to other areas.

PAULA STEPHENS, MA

WELLNESS FOR YOUR WHOLE SELF

Just like in the boardroom, there are many parts to you. What are the different parts of yourself that you identified? It's important to pay attention to all of those parts as we look at wellness.

I like to use the definition of wellness that is characterized by five dimensions. Each contributes value to your overall sense of well-being. It includes your physical health, but it's also much more than that. These dimensions are interconnected to create you—the whole person!

It is important to reestablish balance to your state of wellness after a loss, as the death of a loved one usually impacts all of these areas:

- Social: Your ability to create healthy, nurturing relationships with those around you that help you feel connected.

- Physical: Your ability to get through your day-to-day activities with ease or without undue fatigue.

- Intellectual: Your desire to seek knowledge, be open to new ideas and creativity, and enhance your quality of life.

- Emotional: Your ability to be aware of and accept your feelings as well as cope with life in a constructive way that leads to a positive outlook.

- Spiritual: Your ability to find meaning in life's events and live a life that reflects the values and beliefs that give your life purpose.

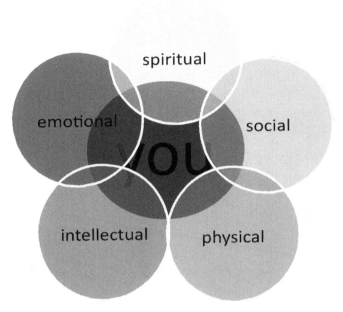

The five dimensions of wellness are all interconnected, with each component relating to another. Each of us may have a different way in which we emphasize or represent these areas. For example, when you are in school, you may emphasize the intellectual and social aspects more, but in the larger picture of our overall sense of well-being, each of these areas is a vital part of giving meaning to our lives.

In this chapter, we are going to explore the importance of the mind-body connection with an emphasis on the important role your physical health plays in your healing after loss. As you read the remaining chapters you will see how all of the Elements of Action each have a place in your total sense of well-being.

In the research I've done in the last couple years, this quote by Bessel van der Kolk, author of *The Body Keeps the Score: Brain, Mind, and Body in the Healing of Trauma*,[9] sums it up nicely. Although I would replace the word "change" to "integrate."

> *"In order to change, people need to become aware of their sensations and the way that their bodies interact with the world around them. Physical self-awareness is the first step in releasing the tyranny of the past."*

As we go into this element, I want to clarify how I define wellness and its integration with the other elements.

I use the terms wellness and self-care interchangeably and it's important to know that in no way am I referring to "cosmetic" fitness. This is not about weight loss—unless it is necessary to treat a health condition, before and after photos, or what you look like on the outside. It's about what taking care of yourself does for you as a whole person.

When I talk about wellness and self-care, these are just a few things you could do for yourself:

- Exercise in whatever way makes sense to you. Taking 3-5 mindful breathes can feel invigorating.

- Eat foods that make your body feel good. Notice how your energy changes when you eat a fruit or vegetable versus a handful of chips. The chips might be an emotional response, whereas the fruit actually shifts your physical energy for the better.

- Get the right amount of rest. Sleeping too much or too little can be problematic. Setting your timer for a ten-minute power nap can sometimes take the edge off.

- Go outside. A few minutes of fresh air, sunshine, and Mother Nature can create a major shift in your energy and break you out of a funk.

Why should you do these things? Because movement will release endorphins, which helps your brain find happiness more easily. Because adequate rest will help you have clearer thoughts and be able to deal with grief easier. Eating good foods will help your body feel better, which will help lift up your spirits. Beyond that, they create habits that get you back into living life again.

THE LIST

Of everything I've shared, it might surprise you that this component of wellness and self-care is the one that literally saved my life. Because my Runner self had already manifested, I had a good habit in place. Then, running kept me on a path away from a downward spiral and toward healing.

One of my friends, Dottie, would make me run every Saturday morning. The gig was, she would text me on Friday night and let me know what time she would pick me or where we would meet to run. It had become a habit, so it just felt natural to always be there.

But when I got her text on one particular Friday night, I hesitated before replying. I was trying to come up with a good enough reason for not going. I wanted her to just leave me alone, but

I began to fear that if I turned her down, she, my husband, or other friends might think something was off. Because something was definitely off.

You see, I was deep into strategizing the next (last) 24 hours of my life. I was so far gone that I had started making The List. It was a list I kept in my purse about the things that needed to get done, plans that had to be executed, and all the other details of how I was going to take my own life, who I wanted to write letters to, and even that I wanted to have my laundry done. Including right down to the fact that "it" had to happen when my in-laws were in town so that my husband, Scott, would have immediate support.

Sure, there were a few things on The List that weren't quite done on this particular Saturday, but I felt that I couldn't hold on any more—my grief had consumed me and there was no way out, or so I thought. Thankfully, I couldn't think of a good enough excuse to text to my friend and tell her I wasn't going to run with her that Saturday. Because I had been practicing this self-care of running long before Brandon died, and my friend helped me make sure it was a habit, I went on the run.

I met Dottie in the parking lot of a common running trail that meanders up a canyon along a river. I can remember that day like it was yesterday, sitting in my car waiting for her to show up and having the thought to act normal—not too happy, not too sad—just be normal. I also had anxiety about getting this run done. After all, I had a list of things to get done that day! I wanted to take all my clothes to the Goodwill so Scott wouldn't have to do it and get the house cleaned up a bit since my mother-in-law would be there after "it" happened.

In the process of this self-care of running, some interesting things happened beyond the realm of exercise.

We went a few miles up the canyon and by chance we ran into a woman who I hadn't seen since Brandon died. As she spoke her condolences, but I couldn't make eye contact so I turned my back to her and leaned over a bridge while she and Dottie continued to chat for a couple minutes. I was anxious and all I could think was, *Stop chatting. I've got shit to do and this bridge isn't high enough to jump from!*

Sometimes people are placed in your path for a reason, and when you are grieving you must recognize that it may not even be because of something they can tell you. It may be for another reason entirely. Just trust it. Finally, my friend and I turned around and headed back to the parking lot.

The next memory I have of that day is sitting in my car again at the trail head with my hands on the steering wheel, taking a deep breath and thinking, "Okay, I think I can make it through today." Because of running and my running buddy, I felt a shift in my energy. I didn't reach in my purse to get The List, and oddly I felt good enough to put all those thoughts aside for the time being. No, I didn't throw The List away, I knew executing it was still an option, just not that day.

The same thing happened to me a few months later while at work. At the time, I was the coordinator of a large fitness and wellness program, and occasionally I would have to step in and teach a fitness class. Again, the stars had aligned and the timing was right to execute The List, although I had added a few things to the list by this point. But on this day, an instructor called in at the last minute to say she couldn't teach her spin class, so I jumped in my car and drove to the recreation center to teach it.

Again, sitting in my car in the parking lot, this time I was fueled by deep anger about how awful everything was and that people would talk about how I seemed so normal when I taught the class that day. I was fuming! I would rather be working on my list! But I exercised and threw everything onto the gym floor. And again, I returned to my car an hour later, sat down, took a deep breath and thought, *Ok, I can make it through today.*

I later realized that for me, exercise was the most powerful anti-depressant. It could nudge the needle just enough for me to make it through just one more day—it was incredible. That said, even with my dear friend's help, I sometimes let my grief decide whether or not to move my body—the one thing that would help the grief. Although sometimes grief wasn't the decision maker, it always said no.

ADDING DEPRESSION

I wish I could tell you that having a Master's degree in exercise physiology and being a wellness coach, personal trainer, and yoga instructor helped me connect the dots quicker, but it didn't. It would take the most serious disagreement Scott and I have ever gotten into—18 months after Brandon died—for me to realize that I was a danger to myself.

From an educational and intellectual perspective and a neurochemical viewpoint, I knew how powerful exercise was, but it was not something I could always apply to my own life. As a person who had never struggled with depression and had built an entire career on the benefits of living healthy, it was incredibly difficult for me to see myself as someone who would benefit from medication.

During one particular appointment with my therapist, she said to me, "If you want to continue to tell me that you're using exercise to combat depression, then you should probably start to exercise consistently." It was one of the many appointments I left calling her every name in the book and swearing never to go back. But she was right.

Exercise works to support your natural balance of neuro-chemicals—if you actually exercise!

As far as the brain is concerned, grief is similar to a chronic state of stress. This quote by John Ratey, author of *Spark: The Revolutionary New Science of Exercise and Brain*[10] summarizes one of many reasons exercise is one of the most powerful tools in your grief tool box:

> *"At every level, from the microcellular to the psychological, exercise not only wards off the ill effects of chronic stress; it can also reverse them. Studies show that if researchers exercise rats that have been chronically stressed, that activity makes the hippocampus grow back to its preshriveled state. The mechanisms by which exercise changes how we think and feel are so much more effective than donuts, medicines,*

> *and wine. When you say you feel less stressed out after you go for a swim, or even a fast walk, you are."*

I want you to take particular notice of the reference to the hippocampus becoming "shriveled" as a result of stress. Not to get too sciencey, but one major role of the hippocampus is to regulate emotions and memory. This helps explain what many of us experience as "grief brain."

In the year after Brandon died, it was almost a weekly occurrence that Daniel would lose his car keys, run out of gas, lock his keys in his car, lose his phone, get in a fender bender and any number of incidences related to an overworked hippocampus. So, if you've experienced "grief brain" you can now understand why it is beneficial to go out for a walk to clear your head! It helps to re-stimulate those areas that aren't working so well.

But many times it isn't enough. Our chemicals are too imbalanced and they need more help. I finally chose to go on antidepressants. Although it was difficult to admit that I was not moving through my grief, starting medication was the best thing I did for myself. It helped me to be able to do other things, like exercise, that helped me deal with grief.

I stayed on the antidepressants for almost four years. When I had built into my life much of the framework I talk about in this book, I felt it was time to see if I could live with my grief without the support of the medication. It was important to me to feel like I could go off of them, but I was also open to the idea that perhaps something had changed in me that would always need them.

I didn't share these stories with anyone for over four years. When I shared them with one friend, she started laughing and said, "Thank God Brandon kept adding stupid stuff to your List, like getting your laundry done and having the house clean. He knew what he was doing!" I couldn't agree with her more.

What I also found out later was my husband and best friend, Beth, had been my secret guardian angels talking to each other and making sure I was always safe.

I don't believe that grief is a type of depression; I think depression and grief are two distinct conditions. But I do believe that grief can eventually lead to depression, particularly if other environmental and genetic factors are favorable to that result. I think it's also important that you understand I believe that 100 percent of people need to utilize good self-care during grief healing, and that there is nothing wrong or shameful about knowing when it's the right time to use a pharmaceutical intervention that will enable you to continue healing.

Once I was emotionally healthy enough to begin connecting the dots between what I'd spent 25 years studying in the field of health and wellness and my own person journey of grief healing, I was amazed by the truth of the mind-body connection. But I also reflected on what it took me, a person with a career in the wellness field, to come to that conclusion. And, if it was that hard for me, how could a person without that knowledge ever be convinced of the powerful emotional healing that could occur through the use of our bodies?

Our cultural mindset about why we exercise our bodies—for cosmetic changes and to look better on the outside—does not encourage us to consider using exercise to also *heal our minds*. Not only that, but in the grief community, exercise is not always talked about as a critical part of the healing process.

Grief is a powerful emotion and one we often don't feel like we have any control over. One minute you're putting bananas in your grocery cart and the next minute you're brought to your knees, crying in the ramen noodle aisle knowing you will never again get to buy those crappy 'hot & spicy' MSG bowls in the horrible Styrofoam bowls for your son. *Damn you, ramen noodle aisle!* Someday I'll get brave enough to buy the horrible bowls of MSG just because I want to have a Brandon moment. I won't eat it, I just want to have it in the house. This is one way I am paying attention to my grief.

And since I've maintained my running program throughout my grief, if I do have a meltdown in aisle five, I can abandon my cart and go running from the grocery store without breaking a sweat or getting short of breath. Ok, I'm joking about that last part—sorta.

The tools that self-care and wellness bring to your grief toolbox are not being able to outrun your grief—I've tried, it doesn't work—but rather it creates a physical system that works to support your process and becomes a tangible way of checking in with your grief.

Let me share with you a visual that I think will help you understand how improving your self-care will enhance your ability to manage your grief.

ENERGY BUCKET

I want you to image that every morning you wake up with a bucket full of water that represents your energy and will power everything you need to get done that day. We all have a finite amount of willpower and a finite amount of energy each day.

The activities that we do poke holes in the bottom of that bucket and let the energy run out. If you exercise, poke a little hole in that bottom of your bucket; some of your energy is going to drain out. Let's say you're dieting, and dieting requires willpower, so you poke a hole in that bucket; some of your willpower's going to drain out. Now put a hole in the bucket for work, family obligations and least we forget—your grief.

For those of us grieving, there's already a hole in the bottom of the bucket. Depending on your type of loss and how recent it is, this could be a small trickle or massive undercurrent that sucks everything out with it; but grief is going to get the first cut of your energy and willpower. If you're not sleeping or sleeping too much, your bucket of energy is being depleted even more.

Now keep the bucket analogy in mind as I describe a vicious cycle that dozens of clients have shared with me about their self-care while grieving. They don't sleep well at night, possibly only getting a few hours of quality sleep. Then they get up and drink twice as much coffee as normal in order to kick their butt out the door to work. The caffeine wears off and the fatigue sets in right after lunch, so to make it through the rest of the day they prop themselves up on either caffeine or sugar—coffee, soda, energy drinks, candy, or all of these.

By the time they get home, they have crashed. They are exhausted and filled with anxiety that they won't be able to get a good night's sleep again. So what do they do? Finish off the day with a night cap—a glass of wine, beer, or emotional eating. Nothing is able to bring you back up again, and so you start the cycle all over again, day after day. This can then lead to other health issues, which can be called secondary losses.

Just getting through the day takes herculean strength; and the worst part is your bucket was empty before you began! Now maybe you don't do all these things, but your bucket does have a few more holes in it if you are grieving. So what are you doing to compensate for that ongoing hole in your bucket of energy?

The cycle is not a sustainable model for managing your grief or treating yourself with the loving kindness you deserve. This is barely surviving and not building any internal structure of listening to what your broken heart needs or using self-care to support your process. Truth is, I've been there. It physically feels horrible and compounds the emotional effects of grief to the point of getting physically ill.

There's so much we can't control about grief, but the one thing we can control is how we take care of ourselves.

I realize it's a really hard to feel like you're worthy of this kind of love and that you're worthy of the effort. In early grief, everything is already such an effort, but remember you are also learning to integrate your grief by giving it a job. Wellness and self-care is good work for grief.

Secondary Losses to Quality of Life

There are many secondary losses that can happen and are often talked about after the death of a loved one. For example, the secondary loss of financial status or income because the primary bread winner dies, or loss of confidence or future dreams. But the secondary loss to your health status can have financial implications as well as contribute to loss of future dreams and self-confidence. Health problems poke another hole in your bucket of energy.

A study published in 2012 by the American Heart Association stated[11]:

> *"Heart attack risks are extremely high for the bereaved in the days and weeks after losing a loved one. The first day after a loved one died, heart attack risk was 21 times higher than normal, which declined progressively over the first month. Friends and family of a bereaved person should watch for heart attack signs and help him or her maintain their medication regimen."*

In my work as a wellness coach for the bereaved, weight gain is probably the most common change in health status, but I've also seen frequent diagnosis of hypertension, auto-immune disease (such as fibromyalgia), type II diabetes, and sleep apnea. Let's break this down and see how this might look.

69

Let's say you're not feeling well, so you go to the doctor and the doctor diagnoses you as having hypertension, otherwise known as high blood pressure. Now you've got to make regular visits to the doctor; that's a drain on your energy. In addition, you have to make a trip to fill a prescription, remember to take your medicine, and you have an additional financial burden of paying for the medication. These types of things continue to drain our energy and we suffer the loss of quality of life because now we don't have the energy to be with our grief, do activities that we enjoy, or spend time with the people we love.

The worse you feel physically, the less able you are to get clear about how you're feeling with your grief because *everything* feels crappy—you're tired, you're lethargic, you're achy, you have no energy, your stomach hurts because you eat too much or you don't eat enough, or whatever that looks like for you. With all of the other stimuli going on in your body, pain receptors and everything else that's happening, how can you open a space for your grief and say, "Here's my grief. How does my grief feel right now, and what do I need to do to tend to it?"

You can't, because your grief is being surrounded by all this other physical manifestation. So before you can deal with your grief in a healthy way, you have to take care of yourself. You need to cling to the idea that wellness will help heal you in more ways than one; so you must be really good with your self-care: taking care of your body, eating right, sleeping well, drinking water, exercising, and moving.

Doing these things allows us to process our grief better. It actually allows us to grieve better, be healthier, and move through tough times in our grief.

THE BASICS

Let's take a look at Maslow's hierarchy of needs.[12] It will help us tie together the need for fundamental wellness in our grief process. Maslow suggests that we all desire to reach our highest potential as human beings, and if we want to progress towards that goal, we must meet certain needs as we go. This is a dynamic model that allows life to happen and movement between the levels is natural.

Maslow's Hierarchy of Needs

When all is going well, most people have at least reached an acceptable level of "Love & Belonging" and possibly even beyond. Unfortunately, when we lose a loved one, we might have to go back and rebuild certain aspects of our pyramid.

When I say fundamental wellness, I'm not talking about what you look like on the outside or following the latest diet or exercise trends. I'm suggesting that you get back to the basics of loving your body so it can work with your mind to integrate and process your grief. As we rebuild ourselves after our loss, it only makes sense to start at the bottom.

SLEEP

The coroner speculated that Brandon's estimated time of death was around two to three in the morning. Even before that information was given to me, from the first night after he died I would wake up between two and three in the morning. I still struggle with sleep and the two to three internal wake-up calls I get. It's usually riddled with anxiety over something I can't control.

Sleep plays an essential role in hormone regulation and many other physiological factors in our lives. Make it a priority to get enough sleep on a regular basis. We are all individuals, but most us of need between seven to nine hours of sleep each night. Be mindful that, although you might fall asleep faster after a glass of wine or a beer, it will take you longer to settle into *quality* sleep, and you might not feel rested in the morning.

If you are having trouble getting to sleep or staying asleep, or you suspect you might have a sleeping issue, talk to your doctor. Without good quality and quantity of sleep, achieving the other basics will be difficult. Sleep is a huge part of your wellness and self-care.

EATING AND DRINKING

Who would think that drinking water would have anything to do with supporting your grief? But it does. Water reduces mental fatigue and can support you in avoiding the "comfort candy" bender in the afternoon by making you feel more full and satiated. So before you go attack the vending machine, drink a glass of water. A good rule of thumb is to try to consume half your body weight in ounces of water each day (i.e., a 150-pound person should drink 75 ounces of water).

When we are down, why do we crave comfort foods so strongly? I think John Ratey, from his book *Spark: The Revolutionary New Science of Exercise and the Brain*,[13] starts this conversation well.

> *"After a stressful event, we often crave comfort food. Our body is calling for more glucose and simple carbohydrates and fat... And in modern life, people tend to have fewer friends and less support, because there's no tribe. Being alone is not good for the brain."*

In this passage, Ratey alludes to the connection between our human relationships and our connection to food. We are hardwired for survival. So when all the other levels of Maslow's hierarchy fall away, we are left to default to basic survival. As such, our bodies will crave sugar and fat to keep us alive. If I had a dollar for every pound of macaroni and cheese I've eaten in the last five years and another dollar for all the chocolate I've mowed through, I would be rich beyond my wildest dreams!

I want to point something out to you before you think I'm giving you an all-you-can-eat pass at the buffet. Yes, your heart may feel broken and you feel lonely. No, your very survival as a human being is not being threatened in the primal way your biology is causing you to act.

When you feel this urge to consume comfort foods, this should be an alarm bell that something is not right emotionally. It's a signal that your grief is trying to take over the boardroom again. Instead of feeding it in the way it is telling you to feed it, you need to hit the pause button. Take a few deep breaths and see if you can figure it out...before you finish an entire box of Thin Mints (not that I've ever done that...OK maybe only a lot!). When this happens, go back to Chapter 1 and see if you can identify what age your grief is acting when you feel like this and treat it as you would someone that age.

Because you have that hole in your bucket, I don't recommend dieting in the way that people typically interpret that word. What I do suggest is focusing on making better choices by taking baby steps. Begin to notice the energetic and emotional difference between cookies and an apple. How does each feel as you let it nourish you? How do you feel after you've eaten? What feels like positive energy and what feels like negative energy?

I recommend journaling what you eat and also how your body feels. I promise you will start to see trends; and when you start making those connections, it will be easier to choose what makes you feel well. That is a huge step toward good self-care.

MOVEMENT

Imagine your grief feeling heavy and thick as you carry it around with you. Now imagine that it's like the tank on a cement mixer truck. The big tank has to keep moving, because if it stops moving, the cement that is in the tank turns to concrete and hardens.

You need to keep moving and keep churning that grief around so that it doesn't turn to concrete; because as soon as it does that, you're stuck. Now, it's not impossible to get out of that place, but it's a lot easier to work with the cement when it's soft and malleable and you can spread it, move it, and create things with it. Once it turns to concrete, you've got to go in there and chip away at it with a jack hammer, which makes it so much more difficult.

One of the benefits of moving your body is that it churns up that grief. Things come up when movement happens—both emotional and physical movement. With movement, we use our lymphatic system, which helps flush out toxins in our body and keeps things clean and lubricated. It also connects our mind and body.

Our bodies know exactly what's going on, so my question to you would be, how is your body keeping score with your grief?

Who's winning? The grief? Is that cement mixer turning and turning, or is it becoming concrete that you're going to have to chip away?

Encouraging you to move doesn't necessarily mean engaging in a structured exercise program. Just start with where you are right now. Moving can be as simple as sitting where you are and taking a breath in, letting it go, then repeating it while moving your arms over your head on the inhale and bringing them back to your sides on the exhale.

The goal is to choose a type and level of movement that meets you where you are and that you can consistently do on most days of the week. Of course there are standards for exercise intensity and duration to achieve specific health outcomes, but that's not within the scope of this book. It's more important that you begin to see wellness as a valuable tool for healing.

Since I was already a runner when I lost my son, it was a natural step for me to use that form of exercise to help me churn through my grief. It was still hard to get out and do it, but I noticed a difference when I did.

Also journal your movement so you can go back and see trends. How do you feel after you move?

MOTIVATION

I've just thrown a lot of information your way regarding action you can take that will enhance your ability to create a level of wellness and self-care that supports your healing. And from my years as a wellness coach and personal trainer, I know that just telling you something doesn't always create change. In this case knowledge isn't power—taking action creates power. But what if you absolutely don't feel like doing anything?

There are many other wellness activities that may be easier for you to do:

- Journaling

- Repeating affirmations

- Meditation

- Artistic creative expression

- Massage

- Hot bath

- Stress management techniques

- Yoga or Tai Chi

Often something simple can shift your perspective and give you the reset you need to take the next step. Wellness and self-care supports our grief not just through our bodies, but also through our brains. If we keep our bodies moving, feed our grief healthy foods, and let it rest, then we can begin to get curious and see what grief looks like; turn it over and inside out. The more we develop a relationship with our grief instead of burying it under emotional eating and a sedentary lifestyle, the more we understand what it means to live with loss.

ELEMENT IN ACTION:

- On a scale of one to 10 (ten being very good), in the last three months how well have you tended to your own self-care?

  - With that number in mind, what one thing could you do that would bump that number higher?

- List three ways you take care of yourself in a way that reduces stress and increases energy.

  - If you aren't doing any, what three would you like to do?

- Set a timer for three minutes. Sit quietly where you can be alone and just observe your breath as it goes in and out of your nose.

- Track your sleep and water for three days. Do you think you get enough of each?

- If you were to make your own wellness pie chart on the next page, how big would you make each section?

  - What do you notice

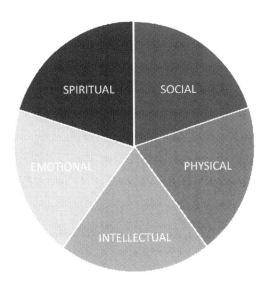

- Repeat the following affirmations at least once a day to shift your mindset:

  - Moving my body allows healing to flow through me.

  - I honor my healing when I honor my body.

  - My self-care is not selfish.

  - I connect to my breath to keep me in the present moment.

  - Write your own!

  _____

  _____

  _____

  _____

3

ELEMENT: LETTING GO OF LIMITING BELIEFS

BirdWings
By Rumi

Your grief for what you've lost lifts a mirror
up to where you're bravely working.
Expecting the worst, you look, and instead,
here's the joyful face you've been wanting to see.
Your hand opens and closes and opens and closes.
if it were always a fist or always stretched open,
you would be paralyzed.
Your deepest presence is in every small contracting
and expanding,
The two as beautifully balanced and coordinated
as birdwings.[14]

I never really understood what people meant when they would say they felt stuck; and feeling stuck is something you hear in the grief world frequently. The poem above illustrates this concept of being stuck by using the word "paralyzed." So often we are clinching down on our emotions to the point of becoming paralyzed, or stuck by our own way of thinking. But when we become present with our grief, give it a job, create a relationship with it, then we coordinate the healing and the growth in a manner that supports creating a beautiful life after the loss of a loved one.

The natural process of grief and loss mandates that we explore all the aspects of what is true about our loss. Perhaps you are, like me, a parent who's lost a child. The deep guilt we feel for not being able to protect our child can be a debilitating wound to our identity as a "good parent." You could also feel deep guilt over the loss of a friend or other loved one, especially if you feel the relationship was left on bad terms.

Reflecting back to Chapter 1, we can begin to look at these negative thoughts and limiting beliefs as teachers with lessons to be taught and as ways to explore our grief and learn more about it. It can open us up to a new way of thinking and allow us to be present in the process.

You may have heard people in your circle saying things like:

"It's time to get over it."

"It's time to move on."

"It's time to put this behind you."

When I talk about letting go that's not at all what I mean. I'm talking about letting go of the limiting thoughts that no longer serve you and do not help move you forward in your healing process.

There are certain limiting beliefs that cause us to get stuck in our healing process if we are not able to recognize them. We must regularly evaluate whether they are still true for us, or if our grief has evolved and it's time to change. If we don't do this essential work of evaluating what we believe to be true about our loss or our ability to heal, our grief might get stuck being a know-it-all sassy teenager. Remember that part of your work is to cultivate a relationship with your grief that is not static, but grows as your grief evolves.

LIMITING BELIEF: NO MORE HAPPINESS

The first concept is letting go of the belief that you can't or shouldn't be happy anymore. This might apply to certain areas of your life that are closely related to your loss, or you might be applying this to your entire life. After the loss of a loved one, it's natural to see how this struggle happens. We begin to think that if we are able to find happiness again or engage in acts that create joy, somehow it means that we're "over it" or we've moved on. We feel like being happy means we have forgotten our loved one completely. Well, it's simply not true.

Take this limiting thought and do this with it—flip it around. Shift your mindset to see that continuing to feel love for the person you've lost (in life or death) can hold the same space with moving forward and pursuing joy in your life after loss. On one hand, I can continue to love Brandon deeply, and I do, but on the other hand, I can be happy. I don't have to be sad for having lost Brandon and remove happiness from my own life. I can hold both of those things—grief and happiness—in the same space.

83

Early on in my grief, I engaged in the limiting belief that I couldn't and shouldn't be happy. It was about two weeks or so after Brandon died, past the funeral because I can distinctly remember it was when I felt like life was "supposed" to get back to normal. My husband, Scott, who works in law enforcement, was working the night shift and I remember sitting alone in my bed at probably nine or ten o'clock at night. The house felt dark and quiet. I remember thinking, "Well, OK, now that I'm supposed to get back to living and get back to life and get back to normal, I guess I've got to figure out this child loss thing."

And so I did what any good person in 2010 would have done. I jumped on the Internet and Googled it. I was sure that, just like when I wanted to run a marathon, I would find a 12-week training program, and poof, my problem would be solved. So off I went to follow the yellow brick road of Google.

I started using search words like "child loss and recovery," "healing," "how to get over it," and "how to work through it." Looking back, I now realize those were such naive thoughts, but when you are deep in grief, you become desperate to figure it out.

I may have been suffering from a little overconfidence; after all I had survived my father's death, my own divorce, and my teenage son's time in rehab. In the meantime, I had laid some pretty good groundwork. I was doing the "have tos" in my life: I had to go back to work, I had to continue being a mom, my life had to go on, and yet I didn't have any idea how that was going to happen. But damn it I was going to find and start the 12-week training plan!

I wandered through the land of Pinterest, reading quotes on child loss and the flying monkeys of other bereaved parents' blog posts. I combed every nook and cranny on the Internet. I never did find that 12-week program I was looking for. Instead, the unfortunate, overwhelming message I got was, "You've lost a child, here's your diagnosis: your life sucks, you'll never be happy again, you'll never get over this, and you'll never find a way through this. Happiness is no longer yours to be had."

Everything that came up resonated as deep sadness and horrific pain; there was no optimism, there was no hope, there was no encouragement.

Rather than pull back the curtain and look for another answer to my pain, I bought it as if I'd been diagnosed with a terminal illness with six months to live. I bought into everything without question. I believed that if that many people on the Internet said life was hopeless and that I couldn't be happy, then it must be true. I took my diagnosis of a whole life of misery and pain and suffering, and I just left it at that.

It's amazing what we allow ourselves to believe. Here I was, searching for hope and I went away with nothing. It just helped to confirm so many limiting thoughts I was having. Without knowing it, I was truly stuck.

About 60 days after Brandon's death, I remember going out to a movie with my best friend Beth, her boyfriend, and my husband. It was a comedy, and yet I cried through the entire movie. I remember driving home and sitting next to Scott, bawling and saying, "I feel so guilty, I feel so awful." And in my mind I kept asking myself, *Why did I do that? I can't be happy, what kind of horrible mother am I?* I just beat myself up because I thought, *This is so wrong. This is so, so wrong. Nobody should lose a child and go see a comedy; that's awful.* After that, I blocked that entire evening out of my memory. In my mind, grief and happiness couldn't exist together, and so I looked for ways to make that true in my life. I got pretty good at blocking what needed to be blocked.

Almost a year later, I drove past that same movie theatre and I had a vague memory of that evening. I picked up the phone and called Beth, "Did we ever go see a movie at Riverpoint?" I asked. Beth, as she has always been ever so patient with my grief, said, "Yes, we saw *Little Fockers*; you cried through the entire movie. It was horrible, I felt so awful."

I got to thinking—why did grief do that to me? Why did it not let me feel any joy during a funny movie? Why did I let grief run the show that day? *Is it possible to have grief but also have joy?*

The answer is a great big YES!

It's really important to find a way to hold both grief and joy as we move forward in our lives. We can and should have both. Grief is a tough teacher and will be with us for a lifetime, but we can have both the love and grief for our loved one AND be happy and find joy in the world. It took me a long time to get on the other side of changing the limiting belief that you can't have growth, and that grief and happiness cannot coexist. But that belief is wrong.

Grief and happiness can both be at the board meeting together. You just have to know how to manage them in the same room.

Almost two years after Brandon died, we took a family cruise. It was the first real vacation we'd taken since Brandon had died. On the first day, once we were away from the pier and into the massiveness that is the ocean, I stood at the back of the boat and bawled. I so deeply wanted Brandon to be there and experience that with us. I wanted to see his face light up with his Kool-Aid grin at how incredible this was.

I wanted to watch the playfulness he never grew out of and see him explore the ship with Sam, who was four at the time. But I also wanted to experience those things through Daniel, Jason, and Sam's eyes. I wanted to see them giggle at the wonder of being on a floating city, so I had to learn how to hold both of those feelings, but in separate spaces.

These are the perfect moments to call on your board of directors. Grief will be eager to step up and shout its injustice at being robbed of the moment with the loved one. But who else needs to be invited to speak up? In the example of the family cruise, the Bereaved Mom part of me was very upset to have this experience without Brandon.

When we took the cruise, my Mom was 84 years old and we invited her to join us. Having my Mom there allowed the Daughter part of me to be present. I invited this Daughter part of me to weigh in about what was important in that moment. She suggested it could be the last time I got to enjoy time with my Mom and to create and share memories with her. If I had only listened to my Bereaved Mom part, I would have been living in a version of life that didn't exist. But if I only listened to my Daughter part, I wouldn't have acknowledged the pain of Bereaved Mom. Honoring both of these were important perspectives to have in that moment and contributed to being able to hold both grief and happiness.

On that trip, looking forward to creating these memories with my other children and with my mother did not mean ignoring the sting of Brandon's absence. I had finally allowed grief and happiness to exist at the same time! I felt such peace knowing I was allowed to miss Brandon's presence at the same time as I was feeling the joy of being with my living family.

Happiness after loss Is a hard fight and you may always feel the twinge of guilt and grief tugging at your heart when you feel new moments of joy. Feeling joy does not mean you don't also have the right to feel grief and sadness, and it's not a reflection of how much you loved the person you lost.

You still have a beautiful life to embrace, memories to create and joy to be harvested. As we continue through this chapter, it's really important that if you are holding onto the thought that you cannot and should not be happy because you've lost a loved one, see if you need to loosen your grip on that thought. Repeat these affirmations:

"It's OK to be happy again."

"Grief and happiness can exist in the same room."

"Laughter doesn't lessen what I feel for my loved one."

Limiting Belief: 'Should Be' Life

The second lesson about letting go is letting go of your attachment to the way things "should be." I struggle with this too, as I am still attached to being the Mom of four boys—that are all here on earth! That is how life should be, but my reality says differently. Often we use the element of time as a measurement of how we believe things should be. As in, children should live longer than their parents. As an example, let me tell you how my life should be right now.

Brandon should be discharged from the army as he would've fulfilled his contract. He was to be stationed in Germany, so in my should-be life, he should be married to a beautiful young girl he met there. He should have served his time in Afghanistan, completely unscathed by physical injuries or the trauma of PTSD. He should have been able to have enough money while serving so that he and his beautiful, kind, lovely wife should be able to buy a house here in Colorado, near me so that I can see the beautiful granddaughter I should have (I deserve a girl after raising four boys). Before he left for the Army, he expressed interest in working for the same law enforcement agency that my husband works for, so again, in my should-be life, he and Scott are working side-by-side.

This is how my life should be, right?

Being attached to how things should be is being attached to how you imagine your future may have been, but—and this is the key—without any proof that that's actually how it would be. That's how I saw my life panning out back in 2010, but staying attached to the way I think things should be does not heal me, it doesn't help me move through life, and it's not based in reality.

Focusing on your should-be life doesn't allow you to move forward with your real life.

Since I have no proof that the life above is what I should have, there are many other scenarios that could be possible outcomes of the last five years. Rather than "should be", what I'm really saying is, "I want my son with me NOW." And that's how I fantasize it should be.

The idea of should be is a fantasy. There's no such thing. When you create and fixate on a should-be, you're focusing on something that never could and never would be. The way my life really should be is the way it is *right now*, because that is what is real, and we can only deal with what is real. In this moment, this is how my life should be because this is what it is—this is reality.

I realize that it is tough to hear those words. It's tough for me to write them—I would like my sweet granddaughter! It stings to say that this is reality, but don't give up your fantasy of how things should be just yet. You just need to alter it a bit.

If you stay attached to, "No, this isn't how things should be," you set yourself up for a lot of unnecessary pain and suffering. Flip this mindset from thinking "should be" to thinking "wish." It seems like such a slight way to alter your thinking, but it makes a huge difference.

We can go back to cultivating our practice of holding two feelings or thoughts at once, rather than feeling like we have to choose one or the other. I can say, "Gosh, I wish things were different. I wish Brandon were here. But he is not, and I accept that."

If I can begin to change the way I look at things and work with my reality, then I can focus my energy on my healing process and ways to honor my son. I still miss Brandon. I *wish* he were here. In fact, I *wish* that we weren't even having this conversation. In my should-be life, neither you nor I would have any interest in reading this book and our paths would never have crossed.

The truth is, I'm glad that our paths have crossed and I love that we're connected, because connection is another vital part of healing. Being real with 'what is' is empowering. It allows us to reflect on our healing process and it allows us to be empowered by reality and a forward focus, rather than being stuck in the past of how things should be. I know that's hard to hear, and I apologize, but this is an important part of the process.

Learn to let go of those false beliefs about how things should be or they will chew you up. If I think too much about the granddaughter I never will have, it will eat me up and put me into a very dark, awful place. And for all I know, he would've had twin boys, and I never would've gotten a granddaughter.

There was no sacred promise between you and a higher power that was broken the day your loved one died. No one ever promised you how long you would have together, so no promise was broken when your loved one died. Yes, it feels like a deep primal wound, and it is, to lose such an important piece of your heart. But the reality is none of us really know the length of the relationships we have with anyone. No guarantees. Some of us live a long time, and others' lives are short.

There is a major mindset shift when we are able to use language that reflects our deeper sentiments. When we say things should be a certain way, often what we are really saying (but is often too painful to say out loud) is, "I never thought my son would die before me. It hurts so much not to have him here."

A favorite quote of mine, typically attributed to the late Wayne Dyer: "Change the way you look at things and the things you look at will change." This quote arrived in my life about the same time I learned about AFGUs. Even when your situation is awful, you can choose to focus on the negative or you can try to grow from it. It was during the year that Daniel was gone that I started intentionally prompting myself to ask the question "How else could I see this situation?" and "Where's the opportunity?"

In other words, let go of the limiting thought that things should be a certain way and flip it. We need to be looking at reality as the way things are—we have experienced a sadness and we feel hurt. While it's painful to think this way, it has a freeing power. Instead of avoiding our grief or feeding it lies, we are being honest in a way that allows us to let the thought go out of us and lift the burden of cemented grief.

We have the power to change the way we perceive the experiences that make up our life. When we can pivot our thinking, even if it's just a small shift,we can turn things that are keeping us stuck and causing us pain into stepping stones. Our new thoughts help create meaning from something initially perceived as painful. This pivot doesn't mean we just slump in our chair and blindly accept our loss; on the contrary, it's like mentally mixing cement. It's shifting our thinking and letting go of limiting beliefs by flipping them around. Ask yourself, "What do I gain when I stay attached to how things should be?"

We have to be brave enough to loosen our grip on this attachment to the way we think things should be. This helps us lessen the amount of control grief has in the boardroom and puts our own best self back in charge. That's when true healing can happen.

LIMITING BELIEF: I AM BROKEN; MY HEART CAN'T HEAL

The last part of learning to let go relates to a very strong limiting belief that often comes from past experiences, your perception of your own strengths, or having witnessed how others have worked through the same problem, either successfully or unsuccessfully. It is letting go of the belief that the wound your heart sustained cannot be healed.

It is the "This experience is so profound that it can't be healed; I am permanently broken" belief. This is the belief that, even if you tried, there is no way through this experience, you can't heal from this loss, and this is one of those life experiences where you are forever broken and nothing can move you forward. The only solution is to just give up.

PAULA STEPHENS, MA

I believe there are tragic, unexpected life experiences that forever change us. These experiences can bring us to our knees and make us feel as if we've been skinned alive. They deconstruct everything that we were made of up until that point and challenge how we identify ourselves and our sense of safety, love, and belonging.

For me, that was the moment I was told my son Brandon had died unexpectedly. I felt like I completely fell apart. I certainly thought I was broken. I didn't think I could ever get through it. Now, years later, I know what comes next.

What comes next is a new phase. In every moment following such an event, we are reconstructing ourselves into something completely different. The pieces of us are all still there, but they're not put back together in the same way as before.

That process of tearing down and losing an essential piece of how we identify ourselves—mom, sister, father, brother, friend—and how we perceive the world around us, means that nothing is the same ever again. And that is scary. It makes us feel broken. But we aren't really.

Being forever changed is not the same as accepting that you're completely broken and unable to heal. Accepting that belief is a guarantee that you will get stuck in your grief.

Healing does not mean that we go back to who we were before or that our lives look the same as they did before our loss. There has been too much external and internal change for that to happen. But healing from loss is not defined by how closely we're able to reconstruct our before lives. We must define our

94

healing using a new perspective of who've we become because of our loss.

Change is hard. It's unknown. Becoming different can be difficult to embrace, but there is tremendous potential in embracing how loss changes us. Letting go of the resistance to accept our lives after loss can be repaid to us in the way of more satisfying relationships, a deeper connection to our spirituality, and personal growth into aspects of ourselves that are only visible because they were broken open.

Just as loving someone gives us a different perspective on how we want to engage life, death gives us the same opportunity, but in a harsher way that we would never choose on our own. When we've touched the most intimate, tender core of our own souls, we discover deeper compassion and a more intimate connection, even to people we do not know.

For example, I will never forget the morning of April 20, 1999, when the Columbine High School shooting happened. It was horrible to imagine what transpired that day. I was no longer that same person 13 years later on July 20, 2012 when the news of the Aurora Theatre shooting emerged. My response was more visceral and created a searing heat in my core that radiated out from my belly because of my own personal experience of loss rested between those two events. I was a changed person and my heart physically ached for the families of the victims.

Let me put it another, more lighthearted, way. My husband, who I love dearly, is a very dedicated Denver Broncos fan. Because I love him, I have a different appreciation for football than I had before we met. This shift exists out of love, not a passion for football. The same concept applies to loved ones you have lost. Since Brandon was in the Army when he died, I now have a passion for supporting organizations that serve our wounded veterans. This is an example of embracing who I've become because of my loss, not expecting to heal in a way that returns me to how I was before Brandon's death. It also helps me honor him and give attention to my grief.

One of the most profound moments that pivoted my healing process was when I got a letter from another bereaved mom named Mary. This woman happened to be the mother of Anna, one of my childhood friends. This family of four boys and one girl had grown up around the corner from me. I had spent hours playing at their house and riding bikes and I still have plenty of memories of summer fun with them.

When I was in my mid-20s I attended the funeral of Mary's oldest son. He was only 18 when he was killed in a car accident. It was one of the most emotional funerals I had ever attended. The church spilled out with young kids, families and people I had known my entire life. As I went through the ,receiving line after the funeral and hugged Mary, I remember thinking how small and shriveled up she seemed. The heart-break and brokenness of losing her son had literally and figuratively made her and her life smaller.

Now the tables had turned and it was Mary reaching out to me. Mary sent me a beautiful handwritten letter and it was the first time I had heard from another bereaved parent who even remotely included a message of hope or resilience or healing. I don't mean becoming healed, but the process of healing, which is really what our focus needs to be on. In the letter to me she said:

> *Having your heart broken through the death of a child—those cracked heart lines—they're like expansion joints, giving you an even bigger ability to love and care about others.*

I remember sitting on the front steps of my house reading these words and immediately feeling a sense of hope. I sat there letting those words roll around in my head like thunderclouds, taking in the huge potential this message held for me. I also remember bouncing another idea around—that maybe this woman was just crazy and this was an impossible feat. Maybe that's what child loss does to you—it makes you crazy.

But try as I might, I couldn't get that thought to stick because there was a deep vibrational truth to her words. A truth that aligned with the Wayne Dyer quote I mentioned earlier. What would happen if I changed the way I saw this experience? I soaked in the magnitude of her words on my broken heart and this is what I heard:

> *Take all these pieces of your broken heart and rebuild it with expansion joints. Make it bigger, make it able to love and give and engage and be more. When we rebuild it, we assert the power of choice—**we get to choose how we rebuild it**.*

We can rebuild it with superglue, a nail gun and screws that tighten everything down and hold everything together so tightly that it becomes hardened, OR we can take all those pieces and rebuild that broken heart with beautiful, colorful streamers, silly

97

string, glitter, grace, and wisdom, in whatever way we want. So maybe you start out with black streamers and the attitude of a world class party-pooper—that's exactly where I started! But it's a lot easier to trade out for different colored streamers than it is to get superglue out of all those little nooks and crannies.

There is a shift that must occur when we believe that we can heal from life's wounds. The smallest shift begins when we exchange a verb for a noun. Replace the word "heal" with "healing." The mindset that someday we will be healed as if grief were a simple bacterial infection is unrealistic. Unexpected loss is not like an ear infection. If I have an ear infection, I go to the doctor, he gives me antibiotics, and I go home and take them for two weeks, and that cures me. But grief doesn't end, though you change as you go through healing.

As I shared earlier, my initial mindset was to find a training program so that I could heal. My approach was that if I could follow a particular regimen, do the right things and make the right choices, at some point I would be cured of this horrible heartache. I originally went into my own healing journey believing I could be healed, but then got stuck in the mindset that it wasn't going to happen. Along the way, you might think that something must be wrong, because you aren't over it. You wonder why; like me, you begin to think you are not deserving of happiness and that this was a wound that would never heal. That's why a shift in mindset is so crucial.

With the help of Mary's letter, I was able to shift my mindset into one of taking action and recognizing this as a lifelong process that I have control over. To go from "heal" to "healing."

98

This is the essence of approaching our healing as if we are cultivating an intimate relationship with a person. We will always and forever be in a process of healing. Losses that chew at the very core of who we are create a lifelong process. View it as going to the doctor and rather than having an ear infection that needs to be fixed once, having a long-term condition that always needs some level of care.

The diagnosis for life after loss is a long-term treatment plan, so let go of thinking that you can't heal from this. That's absolutely not true.

Change your mindset to a process of healing that you incorporate into your life. It's like being diagnosed with arthritis. It's something you will always have. You can do things to manage the pain and even keep the pain at bay, but it's always there below the surface. When you face the fact that you have it and proactively choose things that improve your health, then your body and mind will reap the benefits of healing.

When you lose a loved one, you are forever changed from your experience, but that is not the same as being unable to continue having a life full of the joy and happiness that you deserve. Your loss will be forever imprinted in every cell of your being and everything that you do going forward has the stamp of loss on it, and that's how it should be because we can create incredible things through this healing process. But you will never wake up one day, dust off your hands, and say, "Well, that was a tough road, but I am glad I'm cured from that loss." That's never going to happen, but amazing things can happen when you shift your mindset from expecting a cure to expecting to rebuild your broken heart with glitter and silly string!

A Change of Heart

I once worked in cardiac rehab. People came in who had suffered massive heart attacks and part of their heart had literally died. The cardiac tissue died, became necrotic, there was a lack of oxygen to that part of the heart because of a blockage, and that piece of the heart died. As a result, that person will always have some level of compromised heart function.

No matter how much rehab they would go through, no matter if they had a bypass or other type of interventions, that person will always be compromised. They will always have to live in a way that honors and recognizes that their heart is forever damaged. It's not going to heal the same.

Now, will other parts of their heart take over? Will other parts learn to live with that disability, that hurt, that part of the heart that no longer works? Absolutely. You too will learn with the changes in your heart, and other parts of your life will have the chance to blossom.

Let go of the limiting belief that you don't have the power to create your own healing. Let go of the idea that you have to move on or let go of your love for who or what you've lost. Let go of the idea of how things should be—it will keep you in the hamster wheel of grief. Let go of the idea that healing can be done in one easy, finite period of time, or that you'll be the same after. In your grief, your job is to find a way to continually

100

cultivate healing in your life and recognize that your grief will always be with you. And, just maybe, your heart will be expanded because of it.

ELEMENT IN ACTION:

- Reflect on what comes up to you when you ask yourself these questions:

    ◆ What story am I telling myself about not deserving happiness?

    ◆ What is the truth of that story?

    ◆ What should my life look like today?

    ◆ Do I know for sure that is how my life would look?

    ◆ Am I healing with super glue or silly string?

- Affirmations to shift your mindset:

    ◆ I deserve joy and happiness in my life.

    ◆ I can hold both grief and joy.

    ◆ I am willing to love my life as it is, not as I think it should be.

    ◆ I have everything I need to heal.

    ◆ Write your own!

    _____

    _____

    _____

4

ELEMENT: LOVING SELF AND OTHERS

"Love is not something we give or get; it is something that we nurture and grow, a connection that can only be cultivated between two people when it exists within each one of them—we can only love others as much as we love ourselves."

—Brené Brown,
The Gifts of Imperfection[15]

Grief can't exist without love. Love is to grief as oxygen is to a fire. Just as a fire must have oxygen to burn, your grief must have love. If you never risk loving someone, you will never find yourself grieving a loss. In Chapter 1, we talked about how love evolves and changes over time, as does our grief. Once we've lost a loved one, we can no longer express love to that person in their physical presence. This forces us to explore and get curious about the new ways we will keep our love alive and continue to express it.

Love, like grief, never goes away, and without a thoughtful, positive outlet, our loving feelings can take a very negative turn.

Grief could be more accurately described as love in the absence of our beloved's physical form, to which we were accustomed to expressing our feelings. Part of the healing process is redefining how we express the love we feel for the person we've lost. As we assimilate our loss into our lives, we need to examine love and be open to experiencing it in a different way. The love continues to exist; it's never destroyed, no matter how hot the fire of grief burns. The love you feel for your deceased loved one can be the very thing to put into practice in healing your broken heart.

I want to share a story with you. It's an experience I had that is unlike anything I've ever experienced before Brandon died.

For the first few weeks after Brandon died, I would have a dream every third or fourth night that Brandon and I would come together in various places—a recreation center, my grandmother's house, by a lake, in a church. Although the location changed, it was consistently the same dream. He would pull my head into his heart space and I would feel this warm luminescence, almost like a white light. He would say, "I love you, I love you," over and over again.

I would wake up crying so hard that the pillow would be soaked with tears. The hardest part of waking up like that was leaving my dream when I could feel the peace and pure love energy between us. I believe his message was to help me understand that loving him was not over; it was reassurance that love still existed between us.

The second hardest part about those dreams was looking in the mirror in the morning after so much crying. My eyes would be

swollen shut like I had gone a few rounds with Mike T
I slept. There is no puffy-eye cream powerful enough ror tnat!

I believe those dreams, in my early grief, were gifts that held the secret to moving forward. It was an invitation to reinvent my expression of the love I hold for him.

Grief challenges us to create new ways of showing our love for the person who is no longer with us here on earth. If we really want to dig deep into one of the most difficult AFGOs of all, we are forced to face some demons that, often times because of our love for that other person, we were able to avoid.

In this chapter, we are going to explore how grief transforms the way we express our love and how this can be a powerful way we heal and give our grief a job:

- Finding a new way to express love.

- Nurturing and growing connections with other people.

- Loving ourselves.

FINDING A NEW WAY TO EXPRESS LOVE

Up until the moment our beloved died, expressing the love we felt was a very physical/kinesthetic act. It was a hug or a kiss, buying a gift, showing up on a special occasion, speaking or texting words of affection, baking favorite foods, or a thousand other ways we say, "I love you."

I remember a time this connection was made for me. My husband had trained for his first marathon and the week before the race,

I put together a fun gift basket with all things a marathoner would need: energy gels, bars and drinks, muscle rub, and a corny bumper sticker about being a marathoner. I'm sure Scott didn't really care that much about the gift basket, but he leaned into me, kissed me on the cheek and instead of saying "Thank you," he said, "I love you, too."

He saw right through all the gel packets, muscle rub, energy drinks, and even the bumper sticker, and knew that this was an act of love.

There are all types of ways we express our love, and when a loved one dies, we are left with a disconnect; we wonder how are we going to express the love that we have for that person. After all, we still love the person; the love didn't die. But since they aren't there in physical form, we are at a loss.

You might find yourself asking, "How will people still know how much I love _____ if I can't do anything for him/her?" This then leads to fear that your loved one will be forgotten.

The lack of a physical form creates the fear of how you will continue to express your love for the person you've lost, since you've most likely never had to find another way to love this person. All of a sudden, we can no longer take our love and invest it directly towards the person we so dearly love.

I've had to work on the hole in my heart where my love for Brandon is. Instead of pouring that love into Brandon's physical being by fixing his favorite meal of meatloaf and mashed potatoes, buying him books on World War II, and spending time and laughing with him, I've had to find ways to recreate that love elsewhere in my life. For me it's taken the form of my Crazy Good Grief work, speaking, blogging, offering retreats, and other ways of giving my love (turned grief) a job.

The important thing in early stages of grief is to find small ways to express physical love to your loved one who is no longer alive in physical form.

A friend of mine told the story of her father-in-law and how he experienced the early stages of grief over his wife's death. Raw in his grief, the husband went online researching physical remembrances of their life together. He looked up their first house on GoogleEarth, visited the website of the local German restaurant they frequented when they were first married, and researched places that were important to them from when they met in high school.

When he landed upon a website selling replacements for old china patterns, he checked to see if the site had their pattern— it did. They had never purchased bowls for their china. Even though he knew he was unlikely to use the china ever again, he knew that had his wife been alive she would have wanted those bowls, so he bought them.

A couple of years later, he moved into a new house and decided not to bring the china with him—and he realized that all that time, the bowls remained unused in their boxes. Still, back when he was still raw from the shock of his grief, buying those bowls had served a purpose: to express love to his late wife in some physical form.

107

Remember that living with loss and grief requires investing in a new kind of relationship with your loved one, just as you did with your loved one when you first got to know them. Early, raw grief is often needier—like a newborn or a toddler—than grief that's been worked with over time, though grief is as different and varying as love. Depending on where you are in your grief journey, you need to take action and put your grief to work. At the end of this chapter, I will give you some prompts to help you do this.

NURTURING AND GROWING CONNECTIONS WITH OTHERS

While it can feel positive and healing to find ways to physically express our love even when our loved one is not with us in a physical sense, it is important to remember that love is the most powerful, boundless, and endlessly multiplying force in the universe. The love you feel for your loved one still has a purpose in the world, and it can still do amazing things.

What if you took that love and sent it out into the world? What if the love from your lost physical relationship was fluid, and could spread to others and build them up in ways you haven't even dreamed? What if your soul is really like a forest scorched by wildfire, and while it looks desolate, the soil is fruitful and fresh and ready for new beauty?

It's scary to think we're never going to have that same physical form of love again with our loved one. What if our love never shines out into the world again? This is the fear that ultimately creates action to keep your loved one's memory alive. It is this

Loving others doesn't mean that we get walked on. It doesn't mean that we don't have boundaries in our life or advocate for what's in our best interest. What it does mean is that we are loving and kind, regardless of what we think of others. This is a really powerful thing. When we are both kind and loving to ourselves and kind and loving to others, it manifests a deep well of compassion. A lovely saying I've heard attributed to the Dalai Lama reflects this mindset: "Our prime purpose in this life is to help others. And if we cannot help them at least don't hurt them."

The beautiful thing about love and loss is that it invites the opportunity to develop a deep sense of compassion because you have truly been through a life-changing experience and are more closely connected to understanding the pain and suffering of another.

Let me share an example of how compassionate actions can keep the memory of a loved one alive. A woman in my grief community lost her sister to a heroin overdose. Her sister was a lovely soul who regularly helped others. Since her death, the sister puts together packages of toiletries for homeless women and hands them out when she sees someone who might be in need of such a thing. There is a little note inside saying it's a gift in memory of her sister. So, when people hear of this act of kindness, or a woman receives this gift, they immediately have a positive feeling towards the woman who died, as well as the sister who is keeping her memory alive. Conversely, if the sister didn't give her grief a job and had let it fester into an angry mess, then that would have become her sister's legacy.

111

Practice extending kindness to others. Let go of resentment, bitterness, and anger that keeps you from healing your own wounds and may also damage other important relationships.

The burden is now on us to shine out love into the world by how we present the memory of the person we lost. By continuing to use our love for that person in a way that is so profound, we are better for having that experience—even if their lives didn't last as long as we would've liked.

AND THE HARD PART . . . LOVING OURSELVES

About nine months after Brandon died, I went out on my back patio in the early morning, and I thought, "I'm just going to sit here and enjoy the warm morning sun." I sat on the back patio with my eyes closed. It was very quiet, and all of a sudden I heard Brandon's voice, crystal clear and near my face, as if he were sitting square in front me, say, "It's all about the love." And that was it—spoken plain as day, and not one word more.

As a novice meditator (that's what I call it when I sit in the sun with my eyes closed), my first thought was, *Holy crap! How did that just happen!?* but, at the same time it didn't feel like there was anything weird about it or that I wanted to open my eyes and see what was going on. It felt perfectly natural to sit with the sun on my face listening to the message Brandon wanted to share.

It became clear to me that he wanted to make sure I understood that his earlier messages in my dreams were no accident. And so I've really held that message in my heart, and I've worked on it from many different angles, including the humbling, difficult work of loving myself.

Our most intimate relationships become mirrors for how we feel about ourselves and how we define our place in the world. These relationships give us titles like mom, wife, sister, brother, husband, and father. For example, when I think of who I am in the relationship with my best friend Beth, it makes me feel good that someone with her characteristics would choose me as a friend, and I know she sees the good qualities in me—sometimes more often than I do. And when I think about some of her most impressive characteristics, like her ability to see the good in everyone and always maintain a cup-half-full perspective, it makes me want to be more like that and believe that I, too, could be more that way.

One of the beautiful outcomes of cultivating relationships, be it with our children, parents, siblings, friends, or a spouse, is that our relationships help us define who we are and how we want to be identified. Through vicarious experiences of love with others, we improve our own self-efficacy—the belief that we can perform a particular behavior or act with positive results.

When we lose one of these intimate relationships, it sparks fear and can cause us to see a chink in our own armor. The fear is sparked by losing something with which we identify ourselves. I have spoken to parents who've lost their only child and wrestle with how to continue on with the title of mom or dad when, in fact, they are no longer raising a child here on earth.

The emotional endangerment to our identity is no different than losing a physical characteristic that helps define us. For example, many of our wounded veterans who lose a limb, have a paralyzing spinal cord injury, or endure a traumatic brain injury must go through a period when their definition of what a soldier is changes and no longer aligns with the person they see in the mirror. Or, a more frivolous example might be, if Fabio, defined by his flowing locks of hair, were to go bald, there would be a disconnect and a required shift of this altered identity in order to integrate this into his new identity of self.

When a loved one dies, we must recognize the potential impact on how we used the existence of that person in this world to add depth to how we define ourselves.

But there is another dynamic that often happens when our self-worth becomes dependent upon the ping-back we are getting from these relationships. When we begin to rely on these relationships to prove our self-worth, healing from loss becomes more difficult. It's important that we talk about the importance self-love plays in healing from loss.

Practicing loving myself in the face of my grief and redefining my own identity as a mother has created, by far, the most significant positive shift in my life. It has also been the most gut-wrenching work! Loving myself is a lesson I find I have to learn over and over again. And I will be the first one to tell you, losing Brandon was the icing on cake—literally, I'm a very skilled emotional eater—to send me into a huge tailspin of self-hatred.

Remember how I told you that grief was my childhood sweetheart? Let's just say grief and I didn't always have a healthy relationship. Although we've come a long way in recent years, some might describe our relationship as abusive. I've already told you that my way of dealing with the impending death of my father was through self-medicating and risky behaviors. But what I haven't told you is that even prior to my Dad's illness I had a shaky belief that I was worthy of love.

Before I was a Daddy's girl, I was—and am—an adopted child. From the beginning, I was imprinted with a lack of being loveable. In spite of the fact that my biological mom, who is an incredible woman, had my best intentions at heart, as did the mother who raised me, self-worth and love is still a primal wound most adoptees struggle with. When I tell you that learning to appreciate my own self-worth and practicing loving myself has created the biggest change in my life, I can say that because I came from a very low point. It was a short trip between my loss of identity as Brandon's Mom and feeling worthless as a human being.

My first journal entry after Brandon died shows how unworthy I felt of love and how I felt I deserved all the bad things that came my way.

> *Maybe this is the lot in life for bastard children. Maybe we are supposed to suffer for the sins of others. Maybe it's the negative energy, from which we are born, that we can't escape.*

Thankfully, I no longer feel this way, but it was an easy place to go early in my grief.

In the months following Brandon's death, I went right back to my self-medicating behaviors that had served me so well when my Dad was dying. I drank heavily and would even leave work in the afternoon to go drink. If I couldn't hit the bottle, I hit the incredibly good Danish bakery one block from my office. I remember sitting in my car in the parking lot shoveling a flaky, buttery, full-of-sugar treat in my mouth and consuming it as if it were a shot of gin...even looking around to see if anyone from work was in the parking lot! Alcohol and food became my emotionally numbing I-hate-myself drugs of choice.

My only saving grace during this period was another, more positive behavior I had picked up along my ride into adulthood: running. Running was the one thing that could numb the pain as well as alcohol, and it allowed the grief to flow through me. At this point, although I wasn't inclined to run on my own, I had my friend, Dottie, who would meet me on Saturday morning and make me run with her. As you can guess, I wasn't good company since I was hung over most mornings, and I have since gained a deep gratitude for her commitment to show up for me. But at the time, I hated her for it!

Unfortunately, after loss there may be resentment, anger, and negativity that comes up—especially if the loss is an out-of-order death or other unusual circumstances. In many situations, it is also common to feel regret or guilt over what you did or didn't do in regards to the person you lost.

If any of these feelings are resonating with you, start the practice of noticing when these feelings cause you to behave in a way that decreases your self-worth or causes you to feel like you don't deserve love or happiness.

I have shared a couple of my self-loathing behaviors, but not loving yourself could also show up in many other ways. Take a look at the list below and see if any resonate with you:

- Purposely restricting food.

- Starting smoking or smoking more often.

- Putting yourself down in front of others.

- Using self talk that is demeaning (ie: I'm so stupid, fat, ugly, etc).

- Risk-taking behavior such as unprotected sex, use of illegal drugs, thrill-seeking activities (without proper safety gear or technical know-how).

- Increasing alcohol consumption.

- Emotional eating by over-consuming comfort foods such as high sugar or high fat foods.

- Negatively comparing yourself to others and always feeling inferior.

Doing the work to learn to love yourself is one of the most courageous, exhausting, soul-cleansing things you can do to begin to let go of the, sadness, guilt, anger, and all of the other emotions that we allow to chip away at our belief that you are not worthy of love—especially after losing a loved one.

Self-love is hard enough under the best of circumstances and when you add in how hard we are on ourselves for what we did or didn't do in the relationship we lost, it's understandable why many negative coping mechanisms are born after the loss of a loved one. Reflecting back to Brené Brown's[16] quote regarding self-love, she goes further to say:

> "If you look at the definition of love and think about what it means in terms of self-love, it very specific. Practicing self-love means learning how to trust ourselves, to treat ourselves with respect, and to be kind and affectionate towards ourselves."

Reflect on the kindness and compassion you feel towards someone you know who lost a loved one. Most likely your first thought is something like, "What can I do for him or her? How can I help ease their suffering?" We fall over ourselves to be compassionate, kind, and loving to others, but when we're the ones who need kindness and compassion, we go to great lengths to withhold it from ourselves, even going so far as to abuse ourselves.

We need to learn (or relearn) to be kind to the healing version of who we are becoming because of our loss, and it starts with catching ourselves when we're not acting with the same love we would show someone else in the same situation.

In many ways these concepts of integrating a new way of expressing love for our beloved, appreciating how loss challenges our identity, practicing self-love and worthiness, and cultivating compassion toward others is the most important work you can do to continue healing your loss and deepen into becoming a more radiant version of you.

If you're not sure where to start, go back and review Chapter 3. The concept of believing you're not allowed to be happy is an example of a way to abuse and punish yourself for believing you are not worthy of love and happiness. You could also explore if, for you, there is a connection between how you think things should be and resentment or anger you are outwardly expressing towards others.

I will leave you with a quote from Brene Brown's must-read book, *Rising Strong: The Reckoning. The Rumble. The Revolution:*[17]

"We are biologically cognitively, physically, and spiritually wired to love, to be loved, and to belong. When those needs are not met, we don't function as we were meant to. We break. We fall apart. We numb. We ache. We hurt others... But the absence of love and belonging will always lead to suffering."

ELEMENT IN ACTION:

- Reflect on what comes up to you when you ask yourself these questions:

  - How has the loss of my loved one shifted my identity? Review the parts work you did in Chapter 1 to help you see where grief might be collaborating with other parts of yourself in a negative way.

PAULA STEPHENS, MA

- How can I be loving towards myself without that person in my physical day to day life?

- In what ways am I treating myself with the same loving kindness with which I would treat someone else in this situation?

- In what ways am I holding myself to a different standard of love and worthiness?

- One behavior I could stop that would help me practice self-love is:

- One behavior I could start that would help me practice self-love is:

- Affirmations to shift your mindset:

    - I am enough!

    - Practicing compassion towards others is an expression of the love I feel for my beloved.

    - My love lives on in the actions I take.

    - My actions are a reflection of my beloved's impact in my life.

    - Write your own!

_____

_____

_____

_____

_____

5

ELEMENT: CREATING CONNECTIONS THAT HEAL

"I suppose that since most of our hurts come through relationships so will our healing, and I know that grace rarely makes sense for those looking in from the outside."

—Wm. Paul Young,
The Shack[18]

Like most things I've experienced in life, I've had to learn the hard way about how to integrate loss into my life. One of the biggest lessons I received after feeling so alone for so long after Brandon died was that grief doesn't have to be lonely. It's only lonely if you allow it to be so because there are actually people who understand the exact pain you're feeling—there are people who have literally been there.

Almost immediately after Brandon died, I took very swift action to begin isolating myself. Unfortunately, a lot of people do this. My mind and broken heart were swimming—well, drowning—in unfamiliar emotions, and it seemed any amount of stimulus was overwhelming. My isolation began as a way to make sense of what felt out of control, but I also felt as if there was absolutely no one who could possibly understand what I was going through. So, with a finite amount of energy to expend, it was more energy-efficient to retreat than to try explaining what I was feeling.

Life has a way of preparing you for what is to come. Back when I was alongside my son Daniel in his struggles with drug use, I never dreamed how those experiences would teach me some of my go-to healing tools for integrating Brandon's death into my life. As I look back on all the people, theories, practical advice, wisdom, and healing work that happened in the years leading up to Brandon's death, it's easy to believe there was a higher power at work making sure my family got what we needed for the upcoming chapter in our story.

One of the most insightful lessons I learned was shared with me by the family coach we hired when Daniel came home. Michael was equal parts wise shaman and gentle butt-kicker. His role was primarily to help Daniel successfully transition into "normal" life, but also to work with the family unit to make sure there was support for everyone. The funny thing about Michael was that I connected with him much more than Daniel ever did. As it turns out, I believe that was exactly the way the universe wanted it to work out. And let me tell you why.

It's funny how flickers of time are imprinted into our memories that we later learn have major significance. One of my first memories of Michael is a time he had come to our house to visit with Daniel. My little guy, Sam, was only a few months old. I remember holding Sam as Michael was getting up to leave, and Sam began to fuss a little bit. Michael threw him a look I will never forget—it was a dark look full of anger and disgust.

It happened in a flash, but it was so pronounced and it was at such odds with the man I thought I was getting to know that it took my breath away. I remember thinking it was a good thing Michael didn't work with babies if that was his reaction to a fussing infant.

Two years later, I would learn what I really witnessed was the raw, fresh, cutting grief of a father who had lost his baby daughter (and almost his wife) during childbirth just a few months earlier, and his daughter would've been about the same age as Sam. It was very painful for him to see Sam while he was still in the throes of his own deep grief.

Then, when we found out about Brandon's death, I immediately reached out to the support system we had in place, but hadn't really used in almost two years. Michael was the first one to get back to me, and in my horrible raw grief, his words were like water to a five-alarm fire. I will never forget standing in my dining room on the phone with him, and him saying, "Paula, I get it. I lost my daughter two years ago." In that moment it was as if he had literally given me a resuscitation breath. My mind raced with questions of how Michael had not only survived, but was able to care for my family while in the throes of his own grief.

To this day when I talk to other parents who've lost children, I say the same thing to them that Michael said to me when we met up a few days later. "I promise you, you will feel differently. Right now, your child is in every thought and every moment. Over time, you will begin to go one moment without feeling your grief and thinking of your child, then two and three moments, until one day you will realize you've strung an entire hour together." It was true and it gave me something to measure and hold on to when it didn't feel like anything would ever change.

Whatever the type of loss you are facing, there are people who share your experience. Like my connection to Michael, there are people who've travelled this path ahead of you and others who will be alongside you. When you find the people who can sympathize with the kind of pain and emotional experience of your loss, it allows you to have hope and it gives you people with whom you can share the rest of your story.

Even though I was learning the value of connection after Brandon's death, I chose not to join a child loss support group right away. The truth is, and I'm not proud to say this, I didn't want to be "one of them." Remember how I went to Google for sage advice? The Google gods told me my loss was horrible and awful and child loss was a lifelong sentence of misery. With that mindset, and already feeling hopeless, it made no sense to me why I would go surround myself with "those people." Never mind the fact that they could have taught me so much and given me so much hope in a seemingly endless string of hopeless moments.

In Chapter 1, I shared with you the idea of Parts Work. One of my parts is what I refer to as my Lone Wolf. This part of me is very comfortable emotionally isolating myself, staying disconnected from people, and doing my own thing. Like all our parts, my Lone Wolf started out as a way to help me navigate the isolation after my father died, but as time went on and I didn't integrate my father's loss well, the Lone Wolf became an easy place to go when emotions got tough. Lone Wolf always made sure that I was protected from ever getting my heart broken again—the way it did when my Dad died—by never really letting me get too deeply connected to anyone.

Most people have urges to isolate themselves in grief. It's instinctual and it takes effort to find ways to break the isolation and create connection. In this chapter I am going to share with you three different types of connections that propel our healing forward, often at light speed:

1. Connecting with a community of like loss.

2. Connecting with friends and family.

3. Connecting with your inner wisdom.

I learned the value of connection the hard way, and I wish that early on someone would've laid out the value of connections for me like I'm doing for you. It would've given me an outline of who to connect with when and what each group of people has to offer. It would've saved me a lot of heartache and hurt had I understood the importance of connection in our healing process.

Healing is a beautiful, sacred journey. As such, you get the privilege of carefully selecting the people who will support not just your healing, but your growth through this process. You will never be the same person you were before your loss—you are in a state of growth and integration. As a result, your grief is for the loss of your loved one, but also the loss of your old self. When you connect to others along this path, be mindful

125

of what you need. As your healing journey unfolds, the type of connection that moves you will change. To help you start thinking about how you want your connections to look, let's consider three roles.

1. The Guru: This person is considered an expert in your area of need. It could be grief and loss, a specific type of loss (for example, suicide or cancer) or relationship (such as sibling, spouse, or child). A therapist, counselor or life coach is an example, but it could also be someone who has found another way to be of service and has education, tools, and resources for you.

2. The Big Sister/Brother: This person is someone who has experienced a similar loss, but might be a few steps ahead of you in their healing journey. You can have a mentoring relationship with this person.

3. The Companion: This person provides compassion, walks alongside you, but is also still learning and finding their own way after experiencing some type of loss. They can bring reassurance that you're not alone and what you're experiencing is normal.

You may also find yourself eventually acting in these roles at some point. When we give, we receive, and there is tremendous healing value in sharing what we've learned. Regardless of the role you take and the support you seek, be aware that these are always positive relationships that don't get you stuck in someone else's grief spiral.

Connecting with a Community of Like Loss

One of the most incredible things about being connected to our healing needs by listening to our inner knowing is that it simultaneously supports our connections to others. As you know, I am a huge fan of Brené Brown's work. In her book, *Rising Strong: The Reckoning. The Rumble. The Revolution,*[19] she says this about the importance of connections:

> *"The more difficult it is for us to articulate our experiences of loss, longing, and feeling lost to the people around us, the more disconnected and alone we feel. Of the coping strategies my research participants have shared with me, writing down experiences of heartbreak and grief have emerged as the most helpful in making clear to themselves what they were feeling so they could articulate it to others."*

My favorite part of that quote are the last six words, *"so they could articulate it to others."* Creating a deeper connection to ourselves is not enough when we are up against the huge task of integrating grief and loss. We must connect with others, but we must be somewhat strategic in how we do this so that we receive the biggest return on our investment of time and energy. The second concept of using connections for healing is that of connecting to a community of what I call, "like loss."

Like-loss communities are the people who most closely mirror our own experience in the way we need to express it. It is vital to our healing that we establish a connection with people who get our "after." Once you've experienced a loss, your life is divided into "before" and "after" your loss. Prior to your loss, you had no

127

reason to be connected to these people; they were not a part of who you were or how you identify yourself. You might've even had opinions or judgments about the people who are in these like-loss communities.

For example, if you have lost a loved one to suicide, before your loss you might have had an opinion about the type of person who would take their own life, or what the surviving family members must be like. But now, these are your people—and that's good news! These are the people who are most likely to understand your experience—they get your "after."

One of the reasons support groups exist is that they provide an instant community of people with whom you share a life-changing experience. Alcoholics Anonymous, for example, often becomes more important to a person striving for sobriety than the family members who love them. Although their family loves them and doesn't want to see them suffer, it's their community of like loss that can fully appreciate the struggles and pain of the day-to-day in maintaining sobriety.

You need people—sometimes a small army—who don't need an explanation when you show up, throw your hands in the air, pound your hands and feet on the ground, or hang your head, and say, "This sucks." They just nod their heads knowing what that means in the context of your life experience.

It's also valuable to have people you can go to and share how you're feeling and find out that what you're experiencing or feeling is normal. I have a group of friends with whom I can let my guard down, make irreverent comments, and make jokes about my situation that would make outsiders bristle and feel uncomfortable.

A like-loss community could be a local support group that meets live on a weekly or monthly basis, but it could also be a Facebook group or other online community. And you can expect to have to try a few before you find the one that fits you perfectly. A little bit like Goldielocks!

For example, I have gotten to know an incredible mom who lost her son in a very public mass shooting. Her situation is so unique and multi-dimensional she could fit into many different types of like-loss communities—child loss, gun violence, loss to murder, etc. She has had to be very selective about the communities she becomes involved with, in part because of the public nature of her situation, but all of what makes this so complicated is also the very reason finding a community who understands her "after" is essential to creating the support she needs to move forward.

Another example is of a woman I recently met who had lost her veteran husband to suicide. For the first couple years after her husband died, she attended a support group for suicide loss. She said that at first she felt like, although they weren't military, she needed the support of people who understood the uniqueness of a loss to suicide. After a while she didn't feel like this group was helping her anymore and that she needed something different to continue to integrate her grief. She found a group that provides support for military loss and began to connect with them online and at local events (TAPS: Tragedy Assistance Program for Survivors). In this group she said she felt

129

more connected with people who had also lost a person who had served in the military. And, who knows, as time goes on, she might need to explore other options.

This woman's story also brings up an essential element of like-loss communities. In order for you to benefit from this connection, it must be allowing and encouraging you to grow and integrate your experience into your life. One of the major complaints I hear about child loss support groups is that they get stuck simply ruminating over how horrible child loss is and don't allow for productive and positive healing opportunities. This was the very thing that turned me away from finding a group for four years after losing Brandon—my initial Google search of surviving child loss led me to some depressive, stagnant, wallowing groups that weren't uplifting. This could be true for any support group, not just child loss.

Later, I found that there were groups that fit exactly what I needed. Evaluating the culture of a group is very important when deciding if it's a good fit for where you are and what you need. Another consideration is where you are along your journey. What you need in the way of support will be different in your early grief than it will be later on. It would be a totally normal progression for you to join a group that feels wonderful at the time, but then over time you outgrow it.

Like-loss communities can also provide you with an opportunity to give back to others who come after you. I am a strong proponent of the idea that helping others helps heal ourselves. I believe that getting to the place in our loss integration where we are able to extend support and share knowledge or wisdom can be a huge turning point in our healing journey.

I would encourage you to begin to use the mindset that arriving at a place where you feel you can give back is an important milestone along this journey. I don't believe we should aspire to heal quickly, but to heal thoroughly. Healing thoroughly means we are self-reliant enough in the healing work we've done that setting aside our own pain to help another doesn't threaten to throw us off course in our own healing journey. Helping another doesn't mean we've mastered our own work or that we are finished; it simply means that we are able to recognize the value in helping someone else along this path.

CONNECTING WITH FRIENDS AND FAMILY

Relationships with friends and family often become treacherous terrain after a loss. What our like-loss communities are to our "after," our friends and family are to our "before." These are the people who often knew us at our happiest and have been a part of our lives for years. We feel like they know us better than anyone. It's easy to make the assumption that, if they know us better than anyone and have been part of our lives for la long time, they automatically know what this experience is like for us. The result in our mind is that they will behave exactly the way we want and need them to and provide us with exactly the type of support we want.

Unfortunately, this is not how it works, and when you expect this you are setting yourself up for hurt. The family and friends in our lives do provide an essential element of support and

131

healing, but sometimes we have to get out of our own way so that these incredible people can support us. Let me explain what I mean.

Too many times I have heard the sadness in someone's voice when they share with me about losing a best friend or about a family member who says something like, "We'd love to have you come for Thanksgiving, but it's time you move on. We just can't take your sadness anymore." I had a mom at one of my retreats share about how a best friend of 25 years just vanished after the death of her daughter. Then when she bumped into at the grocery store, the friend told her to call, "When you're back to your old self and we can have fun again."

Of course I have also heard incredible stories of families coming together and relationships being mended because of the loss of a loved one. Loss often reminds us life is too short to hold grudges and resentments.

My own experience with friends and family has been very positive. As you could've guessed, I was no joy to be around and it's a reflection of how amazing my friends are that I still have any friends at all. Actually, one of my greatest blessings in my healing process has been the deepening of my friendships. My friend Beth and I were always close before Brandon died, and she had been along for all of Daniel's adventures as well. But it was in her tenacity to bear down and hold on to me at my absolute lowest points that has really deepened our friendship. And believe you me—I gave it my best shot to be mean, nasty, and downright hateful in an effort to fulfill my belief that she didn't have what it took to withstand this storm.

At every step of the way, however, Beth kept showing up and providing love when I was totally unlovable. Recently she described how she imagined our relationship during the hardest times. She imagined having a string tied between us and she would let me go deep into my grief—she intuitively knew I had to go there—but then she would tug on the string and pull me back to safety.

Today Beth and I are closer than ever and I am deeply grateful that she didn't run away screaming when I did everything I could to push her away.

I did lose one friend during the process. When I was in the deepest, darkest part of my early grief, this friend lashed out at me over a comment that I made on Facebook. This is a friend I had had for years who knew my family intimately. Her reaction was hurtful and unsupportive. It was painful to let the friendship go, but it was clear she was incapable of providing the love and support I needed to move through my experience.

It's very important to give yourself permission to filter who is worthy of your grief journey.

It doesn't have to mean the permanent end to the relationship, and you can be kind about it, but you deserve to select your team of supporters.

Most of our friends and family mean well and are doing the best they know how with the skills they have. The skills any of us have at any given moment are a culmination of our life experiences. We need to let go of wondering why they can't just say and do the perfect thing—they might not have the experiences they need to allow them to do that.

In addition to expecting others to know what we need, we use OUR life experiences as the reference point. The perfect example of using our own life to scale others' experiences is the comment, "I know how you feel, I lost my dog/cat/goldfish/great-aunt/teddy bear/etc." The person who uses this line is trying to connect with you based on his/her own experience of loss. That is the best that person can do with the experiences they have, even though the comment might not otherwise resonate well with you in that moment.

Be realistic about what your friends' strengths are and how they can support you. Perhaps you have a dear friend who is terrible at being able to sit in the fire with you when your grief is burning hot, but she is the number one person you call when you need a babysitter or a last minute favor. She is showing up in the best way she can; honor that in her and don't make her the bad guy when she can't do what she doesn't know how to do.

Another perspective we need to acknowledge is that our loss can possibly bring up some scary realities for our family and friends, including unresolved grief they may have. The loss of a child, spouse, parent, or friend has the potential to make other people feel weak, defenseless, and helpless. It challenges their sense of control and makes them face their own greatest fears of losing a loved one. For them to stand with our pain, they must touch a place in themselves that could be very painful and they don't want to go to.

I was guilty of being this person before my son died, and I'm sure I didn't show up in the best way possible for friends who needed me. Back then, like your friends now, I had a choice of how much reality I let into my world. But after we lose a loved one, we no longer get to choose the amount of vulnerability we expose ourselves to; the death of a loved one mandates that we step fully into vulnerability and fear. And I'm not talking putting our toe in the water—it's a cannonball-type of immersion!

As I'm sure you've experienced, the death of a loved one can shatter deeply-held beliefs about how life is supposed to happen. When cancer slowly draws the last breath out of a young person or a freak accident happens in less than a wink of the Grim Reaper's eye and steals someone's sister or brother, we have no choice but to inhale the vulnerability of being human.

A while back, I reached out to a core group of friends who went through my grief with me. I asked them what that was like. The answers I got were astounding and shed some light on what it was like for those around me to bear witness to my pain. One of the answers I got was so unexpected that it took me quite a while to process it.

I knew that I had been a horrible person to be around and that my anger and depression must have felt like spending time locked in a cage with a Tasmanian Devil. But what I didn't expect is what one friend shared about bringing up her own unresolved grief. Here is what Shonna said:

> *"As time went on, I felt it was more and more difficult to see you. We had gotten together and talked about the details of*

Brandon's death; I was completely blown away when the description of the night he died was so similar to my brother Ryan's passing. This threw me into a tailspin with my own unprocessed grief. I felt like we were both so very damaged, like we both carried a terrible secret, and being in the presence of one another was a mirror that reflected our secret to the rest of the world. It was unbearable.

Time passed. I think it was as much as a year before I saw you again. It was good to see you and the rawness of everything had dulled. I think I got to get to know you again as the changed person you had become, and I could understand that because I knew I was also changing and that you would understand it, without me needing to explain or even mention it.

Now when I see you I'm so proud of who you've become and you still reflect my own experience but the reflection is that of two amazing, strong women who have been through the fire, true survivors."

Until I read Shonna's comments, it never occurred to me that she and I had lost touch during that time because my experience had brought up her unresolved grief around her brother's death. Lucky for both of us, we have since rekindled a wonderful friendship and she is one of the most deeply soulful, beautiful women I know.

I realize it might not fit with the dynamics of your friends and family to send out a questionnaire like I did—by now my friends expect this sort of weirdness—and ask them what it's like for them to witness your loss experience. The bigger lesson to incorporate is to extend your thinking beyond your own experience. Rather than get angry at friends or family who can't or don't support you the way you need, consider acknowledging that 1) they are doing the best they can do with the experience they have, and 2) your experience might be bringing up unresolved issues for them.

How to Get Others to Understand

You don't. And frankly, it's not your responsibility to get them to understand, and it's not their job to try to understand that which they cannot. Your job is to continue to do the hard work of healing the rest of your life and reap the benefits of doing the work. Their job is to be there only in ways they know how.

Your job is NOT to make your grief journey about what or how other people respond to you. If you want to make it about how other people are reacting, then do that by your own actions. Your authenticity and truth about what heals you and owning your journey will make people take notice—in a positive, cultural paradigm-shifting way.

Being angry, resentful, bitter, and complaining that people don't act the way you want does two things:

1. It prevents you from getting curious about your own process and learning the lessons you need to heal.

2. You create your own suffering by expecting other people's validation of your hurt and healing to be what cures you.

Demonstrate how vulnerability can create deeper empathy for others' suffering by embracing your healing. This journey isn't about changing other people—it's about changing yourself for the better. Work to become a better, more compassionate citizen of the world because of your loss.

Yours is a sacred healing journey, not a Disneyland vacation. Choose your companions wisely.

You could go to Disneyland with just about anyone and everything would be ponies and rainbows. The sacred journey of deep healing decrees that we carefully select our cohorts. For these types of journeys, it's better to have a small group of fierce healing warriors—your like-loss community—who intimately know the battle you're fighting, than a thousand fans cheering you on from the sideline. And the truth is, we need both.

I am not suggesting that you unfriend people who aren't able to stand in the fire with you. Rather, cast the characters in your life story in the roles they can best play. We need all types of people in our healing journey.

We need our friends and family as they are the bridge to our life before our loss. These people can share stories and memories of our loved one. They can help us remember the good times and the tough ones, and they help us remember who we are underneath our loss.

Most importantly, seek to surround yourself with those who can stand in the fire with you. Join a support group or an online community, attend a retreat, or do whatever you need to do to cast the other roles that your current friends and family can't fill.

CONNECTING WITH YOUR INNER WISDOM

Early in loss, the feelings of grief are physically and emotionally so overwhelming that it's next to impossible to feel anything except the grief. As time moves on and you begin to integrate your loss into your day-to-day life, it's important you begin to build space in your life to create an intimate connection with your inner wisdom. Cultivating this touch point will guide you toward what you need to integrate this experience.

Inner wisdom is our internal compass, or you could call it your "gut reaction." Except that most of us only listen to our gut when it's a big decision or when the stakes are high and we forget that our inner wisdom is guiding us in everyday decisions. When we look at the Parts Work concept, our inner wisdom sits at the right hand of our soul's purpose. When we are in tune with all the parts that make us who we are, we are healing, growing, and integrating from a place of authenticity and our inner wisdom helps us determine the best next step to keep us on course.

We all have a map in our minds of where we want to go in life. In the case of integrating our loss into our life, the journey on the map is about navigating life after loss and finding joy again. But having a map and a destination does not guarantee success if you don't have tools, like a compass, that will show you what direction you need to move in order to progress through your journey. Without seeking to connect to our inner wisdom, our map is just a piece of paper with no real value.

My favorite example of the importance of using our inner guidance system is Cheryl Strayed's book *Wild: From Lost to Found on the Pacific Crest Trail*.[20] If you missed the book, perhaps you saw the movie with Reese Witherspoon. Cheryl shares the raw story of how, after losing her mother in her early twenties and self-medicating and numbing herself into almost ruining her life, she sets off to hike the entire length of the Pacific Crest Trail (2,650 miles). She had gotten so completely disconnected from her inner wisdom that she took extreme measures to reconnect to that guidance system and find a way to use it to guide her towards the healing she needed to integrate her loss—and subsequent string of bad choices—into her life now and move forward in a way that allowed her to find joy again.

In the book Cheryl says, "I'd finally come to understand what it had been: a yearning for a way out, when actually what I had wanted to find was a way in." I'm hopeful that you are not so far off course that you need to go for a 2,650-mile hike, but if you do, please send a postcard!

In our grief, we might be tempted to go outside of ourselves to escape. We might be tempted to do things that are out of character to disconnect with our inner wisdom and hide from our sad realities. These instincts occur at times when we need to connect with our inner wisdom the most—when our inner wisdom is gently tapping us on the shoulder and whispering to us what we really need to heal.

Connecting with your inner wisdom starts small. It starts with accepting you already possess all the wisdom and knowledge you need to heal. I know you might not feel this way; I know that your lack of belief in this truth is probably why you bought this book. You probably bought this book because you hoped I would give you "the secret" to a happy life after loss, or because you thought I held some special key that you lack. But I see your desire to heal differently than you do. I see you seeking a way to tap into your own wisdom to do what you already know how to do.

You see, I have this belief that we are only attracted to the things that, in some form, already exist in us. If you are reading this book, I believe that on some level there is a familiarity about these ideas that invites you to explore further because it resonates with something deep within you.

Using this thinking, I want you to begin to shift your thinking from believing that you don't have what you need to heal to believing you *do*—you just haven't quite uncovered it yet. This is a powerful mindset shift that allows you to plug in to and bring to light what already exists in you.

When you are able to carve out intentional space to listen and feel for your sweet, quiet voice of inner wisdom, you will begin to take back control of your life. You will improve and reestablish this vital connection when you engage in activities that reduce outside distractions. You begin to not just give yourself permission to speak your truth to yourself, but also take action on that truth, own it, and bring it to life.

Your inner wisdom has not left you, it's always been there for you. As you begin to explore how to elevate this power for healing, consider how you best receive information. Do you learn best when you hear information (auditory), see it (visual), or use movement to process it (kinesthetic)? Use this type of information processing to jumpstart a conversation with your inner wisdom. Some suggestions to get you started:

- Go for a walk—bonus points if you can get into nature.

- Journal

- Connect to your breath

- Doodle or create art (think adult coloring books!)

- Meditate

Start small when connecting to your inner wisdom, maybe with only a few minutes of these activities. While doing these activities pay attention to the presence of a "gut feeling" or "little voice" that feels vaguely familiar and comforting. As you become re-acquainted with your inner wisdom you will naturally want to spend more time opening up the lines of communication.

A simple next step is to ask it very basic yes/no questions. For example, "Do I need to eat a second serving of ice cream?" Or perhaps you're approaching a special day that would have been spent with your loved one. With a simple yes/no question, ask what your inner wisdom wants you to know. For example, "Should I spend my loved one's birthday alone with my feelings? Do I need family and friends for support?" You will feel the right answer. When you get the answer, tune into how you knew it was right. Was it a feeling in your belly or heart space? What it a voice? How did it make you feel to get the answer?

The other way we improve our connection with our inner wisdom is to reduce the amount of self-medicating and numbing activities that we do to go outside of ourselves. As I have already shared, I did more than my fair share of these self-medicating activities early in my grief. With so many angry outbursts, emotional eating, and booze, my poor little inner voice wasn't ever going to be heard over my pounding headaches, stomach aches, and hangovers! But when I began to lessen the grip of these activities and create space and peace for my inner knowing to speak up, the weight of my grief immediately shifted and I began to find clarity about what I really needed to heal.

When we overindulge in self-medicating activities, we are distancing ourselves from our inner wisdom. Remember that this is our grief trying to help, but we know better. It's a cry for help we must pay attention to. The real reason we do this is because we are afraid of what our inner wisdom will say to us. But our inner wisdom will never tell us anything that will hurt us. Yes, the healing process is often painful and our inner wisdom is our greatest healer, but believe me when I say that avoiding our inner wisdom will lead to deeper and more strenuous pain.

How the Connection to Self, Like Loss, and Friends and Family Overlap

I just shared with you the three main areas of connection— like loss, friends and family, and inner wisdom. These three connections do not act independently, nor do you work sequentially through them; there is definite overlap. This is a good thing. Each one supports the other and as our grief evolves and we continue to develop our relationship with it, we will find the time we spend in each type of these connections is fluid and ever changing.

For example, a woman in my Crazy Good Grief community (an example of like-loss connection) participated in a series of live conference calls I hosted. In one of the calls, we had a guest speaker who shared her thoughts regarding what happens to us after a tragedy and how we recover. Our speaker was a well-respected PhD in the area of growth after tragedy.

A few days later, the woman who was listening emailed me and said she hoped I didn't take offense, but she didn't agree with what the woman had said about how we recover from tragedy. The information didn't align with her spiritual beliefs and she didn't feel it was helpful for how she thought about the topic. What she had done was use her connection to a like-loss community for support and to learn something new, then she had taken that information back to process it using her inner wisdom. The result was a better understanding of what heals her and how she can find support. She didn't agree, but the important part was that she was listening to her inner wisdom.

Although I didn't hear from other people on that call, it's safe to assume that others heard the message, bounced it off their inner wisdom and had a different result. Or that someone wasn't feeling clear with their inner wisdom, but the guest speaker brought up thoughts or ideas that helped clarify something for them.

We need all of these connections to move us through the healing process and we need to be open to the evolution of these connections.

ELEMENT IN ACTION:

- To connect with your inner wisdom, you must reduce outside distractions and noise. List three activities you enjoy or would like to try that calm your mind.

- List the types of like-loss communities you might fit into. For example: groups for widows, sibling support, suicide, military, child loss, overdose death, gun violence, depression, etc.

  - Now research local and online resources that sound interesting to you.

- List three or four ways you can use your family for support that doesn't include them "getting it."

- Affirmations to shift your mindset:

  - My inner wisdom will guide me.

  - I have all the answers within me.

  - I am stronger when surrounded by love.

  - We are all doing the best we can with what we know.

  - Write your own!

145

PAULA STEPHENS, MA

_____

_____

_____

_____

_____

6

ELEMENT: GRATITUDE

"You simply will not be the same person two months from now after consciously giving thanks each day for the abundance that exists in your life. And you will have set in motion an ancient spiritual law: the more you have and are grateful for, the more will be given you"

— Sarah Ban Breathnach,
Simple Abundance[21]

Gratitude may seem like the last thing you want to practice in your grief. Gratitude might also seem like a very trite suggestion as an action you can take that will actually move you forward in your healing. As someone who has made a career in the wellness field, I was familiar with the concept of gratitude in helping a person's total self. But when I began my search for what heals *me in grief*, I didn't believe in the power of gratitude as a practice for healing.

As much as I like the "woo-woo" world of my yoga practice and tapping into my "inner wisdom," I'm also an exercise physiologist. The scientist part of my brain wants to have the science and the research to back up my practices. In grad school, I wrote a very in-depth research paper on the positive benefits of yoga on cardiac rehab patients. Even though I knew and had experienced yoga's health benefits, I still needed to connect the space between woo-woo and science. I am almost always the last one to jump on a fad diet or exercise program because I tend to wait it out until the research tells me more. When it came to my own grief healing, I knew I needed the same dual-minded approach to be sold on the concept of gratitude and its healing power.

A few years back, I interviewed a woman, Toni Powell, who had done a very popular TEDx talk in Australia[22] on the power of gratitude. I expected her to tell me in woo-woo terms how it would make me feel happy and I would learn to appreciate what I have. Instead, she busted out the science and the research that shows how and why gratitude works. I immediately perked up and started taking copious notes! The other part of the interview that made me perk up and listen is that this woman described herself as a pessimist and someone who is not naturally inclined to be grateful.

Afterwards, I began to connect the dots in my own experience. I had not intentionally set out to practice gratitude in my healing after Brandon's death, but somehow these small nuggets of gratefulness started to infuse themselves into my world, and I began to see how my view was changing.

One of the things that we know about gratitude from a scientific standpoint is that when we practice gratitude, and especially if we write down what we're grateful for, it re-molds and rewires our brain. When scientists look at brain activity, the brains of people who practice gratitude light up in a way that enhances all types of benefits, including greater short-term memory and improved immune system.

As Rick Hanson states in his book *Buddha's Brain: The Practical Neuroscience of Happiness, Love, and Wisdom*:[23] "Ordinary activities contain dozens of opportunities to change your brain from the inside out...Both temporarily and in lasting ways; neurons that fire together wire together." I love the last part of that quote, "neurons that fire together wire together." I imagine these gratitude neurons intertwining themselves with other neurons we've cultivated that are not of the gratitude type and holding each other tight and promising not to let go. Our brains change all the time based on the type of stimulus we give it. Your brain is constantly adapting to the input by all your body systems, including the nervous, musculoskeletal, and cardiovascular system as well as hormone fluctuations.

Your brain is capable of what's called "neuroplasticity." In laymen's terms, this means your brain is flexible and moldable in regard to the types of thoughts you have and that you have control over much of the tapes that play in your head. Our brains are always taking in, processing, and assimilating to new information. Whatever you're putting in your brain is what you're hardwiring that brain to be in tune with or sensitive to.

To better imagine what happens in the brain, imagine how your body would change if you were to begin lifting weights consistently. Your muscles would develop pathways that were efficient for the activity of lifting weights, and you could see the change in your muscles and the look of your body as a result.

Our brains do the same thing. Only, you can't see the amazing change that is happening in your brain, but you can feel it in your level of happiness and satisfaction. Your brain will build pathways—in the way of thoughts, behavior patterns, habits, etc.—that reflect the most common information that's being put in.

An easy way to visualize this is to think of how the Grand Canyon was made. A consistent flow of water over a long period of time created a beautiful deep crevasse that is one of the greatest wonders in the world. What you put in your brain is the water that creates the pathways for your thoughts and feelings.

So, as you can imagine, this is true for both positive and negative thoughts and feelings. On the negative side, a study of 100 healthy participants conducted at Yale University[24] showed that those who had experienced a major life stress—such as the death of a loved one—had shrinkage in the front part of the brain. This part of the brain is in charge of things like emotions and self-control, but also physiological functions such as blood pressure and blood sugar levels. This could explain why your grief has made you feel like you're in a fog, forgetful, or slow to process. This connects us back to the element of wellness and self-care, in Chapter 2, when I shared that exercise can help rebuild this part of the brain. It can also support the concepts from that chapter regarding the increase in susceptibility of secondary losses to your health as a result of grief that isn't cared for.

Gratitude is worth so much more in our lives than we give it credit for. And if we incorporate it into our healing, it can help make us more than we could ever imagine.

GRATITUDE: THE ANTI-GRIEF

Here's where gratitude really comes in: gratitude has the opposite and almost reversible effect on your brain from those effects of grief. I repeat: practicing gratitude is the opposite of practicing grief, and can actually reverse some of the negative effects of grieving. When we practice gratitude on a daily basis, when we write our gratitude down (which research has shown helps us retain those thoughts), when we look for opportunities to be thankful, when we recognize good things in other people, when we look down the street and we try to look for the happy people, when we're looking for that sense of happiness, our brain is actually changing.

Because I'm familiar with the inclination myself, I know you may be thinking, *Well, I don't want to change my brain. I miss my loved one and if I change my brain, I'm afraid I won't miss them anymore and that makes me a terrible person.* From one bereaved person to another, I implore you: acknowledge the falsehood in this belief. I encourage you to practice holding both of these feelings. You *can* practice gratitude at the same time as you long for your loved one.

Remember back in Chapter 3 when we talked about what it means to let go of limiting beliefs and hold on to love for your loved one at the same time? I miss Brandon, but it doesn't mean that I love Brandon any less if I take advantage of an opportunity to be happy or I take advantage of an opportunity to be grateful for what I have. As we've discussed before, happiness and grief are not mutually exclusive emotions.

When you start practicing gratitude, if you look for the good stuff, it doesn't mean that you are "getting over it" or "moving on." Practicing gratitude is about taking time to notice the things in our lives that are good—and there are always good things in our lives! But even in the best of circumstances, it takes intention and practice to notice good things. In grief, this practice can feel insurmountable at times. I promise it gets easier. Remember— you're working to retrain and rewire your brain. It takes time!

One of the most precious and important practices in my healing journey has been to take time to remember everything I can about my dad and Brandon. The memories I have of them are like rare gemstones in my memory bank. One of the things gratitude does is enhance memory. When you are practicing gratitude, you can actually be strengthening the memories of your loved one. That is a win-win in my book.

As human beings, our brains tend to notice what we are looking for. When we are looking for the bad stuff, when we're looking for opportunities to say, "See? Life isn't fair. See? Life sucks. See? That person got it and I didn't. See? I'm not here to heal. See? Things are not going my way," we find only the bad stuff because the bad stuff is on our radar.

For example, a couple of months ago, my husband bought a new car. It's a red Toyota. We've never owned a red car or a Toyota, but all of a sudden I see red Toyotas everywhere! I'm sure there aren't more red Toyotas on the road all of a sudden; the difference is in what I'm noticing. The same holds true with gratitude or whatever thoughts you are wanting to find. Once we start changing the plasticity of our brain and we rewire it for the positive, we will start to see more of the good things.

Some of the most profound research out there in gratitude states that the number-one factor that contributes to your level of happiness is your level of gratitude. There is a strong and direct correlation between how grateful you are and how happy you are. In one study, researchers had people rate their happiness, then they had them engage in a gratitude project or activity, and then they asked them to rate their happiness again. The participants' happiness went up between 4 and 19 percent.[25] And the bridge from one state of happiness to a higher level of happiness was simply an act of gratitude.

In another study, researchers assigned participants one of three tasks. Each week, participants kept a journal of short entries. One group was asked to list five things they were grateful for each week, a second group recorded things that had happened that upset them, and the third group made a list of five things that happened to them, but they were not instructed to report specifically positive or negative experiences. Ten weeks later, participants in the gratitude group felt better about their lives as a whole and were a full 25 percent happier than the group that focused on upsetting experiences. They reported fewer health complaints and exercised an average of 1.5 hours more.[26]

Imagine if you increased your happiness by 25 percent. Think of the quality of your life, think of how the quality of your thoughts would change. Another observation that came out of that same study was that gratitude doesn't just make us feel better in the moment we are practicing it, but it has longer lasting affects by increasing our happiness in the future.

Gratitude also allows us perspective to keep us from getting stuck in our negative thinking about how crummy our life is. When we think everything about how our world stinks and things aren't going our way, we wonder why we have to go through this and why we have to suffer. Getting stuck in a cycle of negative rumination can easily happen after we lose a loved one.

The gaping hole in our lives where that person used to be can feel like a spotlight illuminating everything we don't have. This can be the beginning of a downward spiral of negativity that will eventually seep into every area of our lives. This negativity is often the fork in the road that takes you away from healthy grief and healing from loss to a path of resentment and anger. Gratitude is one of the quickest ways to turn that around. Once you quit thinking about the crummy parts of life and fill it with something you are grateful for, then suddenly your dark world turns bright.

GIVING AWAY OUR POWER

I have always felt like anger, resentment, and depression are the go-to emotions that come out of loss. And although they are the often the easiest emotions to access, as they eagerly reside right under the surface, they yield the least amount of positive healing return on investment. They have the potential to completely derail your healing process.

This is not to say that these emotions don't deserve their time in the spotlight. All emotions we have are valuable teachers along our path. Especially in early, fresh grief, these painful emotions serve us well. They are hot, fiery, easy to access, and don't require a lot from you in terms of figuring them out. I see these emotions as wild fires; they come through and burn everything to the ground. The result, in the next season, is beautiful fertile soil ready to sprout tender green foliage in its place.

But one of the problems with these easy-access emotions is that they are not satisfied to simply have your attention; they want to attract the attention of everyone who dares cross your path. These emotions bark out to everyone who will listen to validate their presence and acknowledge their power. Then you, the real person with a wide array of emotions to express, are left dependent and waiting on the validation of others for your pain and suffering.

The reality is the person who most intimately knows and understands your pain is YOU! The payment that anger, resentment, and depression asks for in return for their fiery hot expression is that you give away your power and wait patiently for someone else to authenticate your pain of losing a loved one. The moment you give away your power and rely on external forces to confirm that your loss is painful, real, and life-changing, you have slammed the brakes on your own healing journey.

There is no place with more evidence of this arrangement than social media outlets. As a guest blogger for many online sites, I've noticed that the posts that get the most likes and shares are those that put to words how painful the experience of loss is. I also see it on Facebook as holidays like Mother's Day and Father's Day approach. During these celebrations, there becomes an almost counterculture of memes and quotes about the pain and hardship these days bring when you've lost your mother or father, or you are part of the child loss community. I have seen grieving people dedicate multiple Pinterest boards to the subject of their pain.

I am not against social media or public expressions of our feelings. What I am asking is that you don't engage in these endeavors with the hope that a Pinterest board or Facebook meme is going to shift your healing and support the hard work healing requires of YOU. You cannot shuffle the work of your healing onto others. I would also beg you not to give your power away. Stand firm in knowing that whatever you feel, however your loss has gouged a deep hole in your identity, that it is enough.

There is no one in the world you have to prove your pain to, and a thousand Facebook likes on your meme will not make the pain go away.

In this chapter, I illuminate these easy-access emotions and ask you to notice if you are asking others to validate your pain. If you recognize your own tendencies around this, it will be easier to understand that these habits will keep you stuck and unable to let gratitude work its magic. If you are reading this chapter and find that you can't or aren't ready to let go of the anger, resentment, and depression that you've been carrying with you, and you can't even begin to imagine being grateful for anything in life right now, that is perfectly okay. It doesn't mean you are a terrible person or that you are powerless to integrate your loss into your life. Quite the opposite—recognizing where you are allows you to begin your journey from exactly where you are. This is also the perfect place for you to go back to Chapter 5 and dig deeper into creating your like-loss communities and reconnect to your inner knowing.

Remember that your like-loss communities are the ones who can come the closest to understanding and validating your pain because they, too, are on the same journey. This community will fill your tank and give you so much more than any Facebook post or Pinterest board because these are your people!

Taking the time to check in with your inner wisdom and allowing it to guide you to your next best step takes anger and his friends out of the driver's seat and allows your deepest desires to heal to be heard. If you are still struggling with how to be grateful, combine your inner wisdom with the parts work from Chapter 1. I would also encourage you to review Chapter 4 and learning to love yourself, as it is very likely you are using these negative emotions as a way to punish yourself.

How to Start a Gratitude Practice

My most favorite healing tools are followed by the word "practice." Yoga practice, meditation practice, and gratitude practice, for example. To me, this takes the pressure away from trying to achieve a certain level of proficiency or accomplishment. Compared to my days of running marathons (and trying to achieve a personal record), which were labeled "training plans," I'll take "practice" every time. "Practice," unlike "plan," isn't focused on a destination. That's how I ask you approach implementing gratitude into your life. Let go of thinking it leads to a specific place and time where you will wake up and find you've "healed."

Release the idea that you will be graded on your gratitude proficiency by taking an exam. Gratitude has much more ease to it and the ability to expand and contract to meet us where we are while still administering the perfect dose to heal us. For example, while I write this I can practice gratitude for the sweet bird chirping outside my window and the tick-tock of the clock in my office that was given to me by one of my yoga students. It's not the material possession of the clock, but the connection to the student who gave it to me and that her gift came from a place of kindness toward me.

These small acknowledgments connect me to what is good in my life right here in the present moment. Gratitude doesn't require that I long for the past or desire a better future; gratitude grounds me in what's good in my life in this *very moment* — and I don't have to post it on social media to make it real!.

You can practice gratitude right now as well. Take a deep, full breath and think of something in this moment that you are grateful for. Exhale and let it soak in. If you're struggling, here are a few prompts to support your practice:

- Your lungs are healthy enough to take a deep breath.

- Your ears can hear the sounds around you.

- You are able to read these words and think about gratitude.

Another favorite (and silly) way to begin to infuse gratitude into your life is by playing, what I call, the opposite game. The opposite game is when we find the gratitude in situations that annoy us. For example, you're in a hurry at the grocery store and get in the "15 Items or Less" line, only to find the person in front of you clearly has more than 15 items. Rather than get grumpy, practice gratitude.

- Be grateful that you have an extra couple minutes to relax and breathe before you get on to the next thing in your life.

- Be grateful you know how to count to 15 (do this in a light-hearted way and without judgment of the person in front of you).

- Be grateful you have money to buy what you need.

- Be grateful for the person in front you for helping you practice patience and gratitude.

Remember the goal of practicing gratitude is to rewire our brains to consistently look for the good stuff. So when you play the opposite game, you are tricking the brain into wiring together the positive connections and letting go of the negative ones. Intentional gratitude means allowing ourselves an opportunity to look around and see how blessed our lives really are and to look at the places of life that are really full.

Another tool I use for cultivating gratitude is to dial down and get really specific about what it is I'm grateful for. It's easy to say, "Well I'm grateful for my friends, my family, and the air that I breathe." Those are the easy ones. Think more specifically about why those people or things make you happy. How do these people or things specifically affect your level of happiness? Instead of simply saying, "I'm grateful for my family," say, "I'm grateful for the people who will bring me unconditional love, even when I don't feel deserving of it" or "I'm grateful to have a family who finds joy in doing things together—this keeps me active, and being active makes me happy."

For me, when I think about my best friend Beth, yes I'm grateful for her friendship, but what I'm really grateful for is that she is always 100 percent honest with me. She provides me with a mirror so I can see myself and my relationships clearly. I am also grateful that she and I share a desire to pursue meaningful lives. This common desire keeps us connected.

Remember to just start practicing where you are in your healing journey. If you're in the early stages of grief, I realize this may feel very difficult. Even in the deep sadness of your grief, you can be grateful for the relationship and time you had with the person you lost. Make it part of your gratitude practice to write down the memories you're grateful for.

A wonderful exercise a friend of mine shared was keeping a journal for the first year after her loss. Each day she would write down a memory, glue a picture, or write a quote that reminded her of her loved one. At the end of the year she had 365 ways to be grateful for the relationship she had and could always refer to it for inspiration. Maybe in a few weeks you can think about one thing per day. Eventually you will begin to widen your circle of gratitude and realize the incredible experiences that are right before your eyes every day!

One thing I've noticed that has shifted for me is my connection to nature's beauty. I notice sunrises, sunsets, and full moons now more than I ever did before. I find myself feeling so grateful for these and in turn they change my whole outlook on life.

ELEMENT IN ACTION:

- Start shifting your gratitude mindset with the simple things. In this very moment, take a breath and say three things you are grateful for.

- Keep a journal and each morning or evening. Create a habit of writing down three to five things you are grateful for.

- Be creative and make it a game: How many people can you count today who are smiling? Bonus points if they are by themselves with apparently no reason to smile!

- Try to smile at every stranger you meet today.

- Call a friend and tell them you appreciate their friendship. Notice how good it feels to make someone else happy.

7

FINDING YOUR EMPOWERED PURPOSE

"The art of life is to stay wide open and be vulnerable, yet at the same time to sit with the mystery and the awe and the unbearable pain – to just be with it all."

—Ram Dass,
Polishing the Mirror[27]

Healing does not mean that we go back to who we were before our loss or that our lives look the same as they did before. Nor can we define our healing by how closely we're able to reconstruct our "before" lives. We must define our healing using a new perspective of who we've become as a *result* of our loss.

This is a choice I challenge you to make. You have changed at such a deep, soulful level that you cannot physically, emotionally, or spiritually be the person you were before your loss.

The work, as illustrated throughout this book, is not to find an answer to the "why did this happen to me (or my loved one)" question, but to do the healing work that will help you heal to the point that you can create meaning out of something that seems meaningless. This is the work that must be done so that you can create your empowered purpose from this experience.

Empowered purpose is what happens when we do the hard work that healing requires of us and the benefits we reap fill our souls and put passion into our lives. I am equal parts woo-woo princess and hard-facts scientist. Much like what happened to me with gratitude, I needed to find the scientific facts that living a happy life after a traumatic life event was possible, not just some feel-good talk I'd overheard at the meta-physical bookstore.

I wanted to know that life after loss wasn't just about learning to survive the event, but there was potential to use this event to enrich my life and find a deeper purpose to how I was living the one precious life I have. And again, just like with gratitude, I found the science I needed to back up my ethereal thinking about cultivating an empowered purpose. The pain of your loss has cracked open your life in a way that presents a unique opportunity to experience what researchers call Post Traumatic Growth (PTG).

PTG refers to the positive changes that occur as a result of struggling with a major life crisis or a traumatic event. We, as human beings, can be changed by our life experiences in radically positive ways. This idea of exploring the upside of tragedy was originally created by Richard G. Tedeschi and Lawrence G. Calhoun at the University of North Carolina at Charlotte in the mid-1990s. According to Tedeschi, as many as

90 percent of survivors report at least one aspect of PTG.[28] The five most common ways people feel a sense of growth are:

1. You become open to new opportunities that didn't seem present, available, realistic, or practical. This could manifest in your life by going back to school, achieving a long abandoned dream, booking a trip to Machu Pichu, skydiving, or if you're like Cheryl Strayed, the bestselling author of *Wild*, walking the entire Pacific Crest Trail.

2. You feel a deeper intimacy in current relationships or with specific people and/or an increased connection and compassion to others who suffer. I know this is true for me. I can no longer watch the news and hear of a tragic event without transporting myself into the families who are struggling to put the pieces back together. I find I am also much less judgmental and much more accepting and willing to extend helping hand than I was before.

3. You feel a profound increase in your own self-efficacy: "If I lived through that, I can face anything." Yes, a thousand times—YES! Look at how far you've come and how hard you've worked to integrate this experience into your life. Take this new found belief that you are brave enough and courageous enough and have faith that in this you are giving purpose to your loss.

4. You feel a greater appreciation for life in general. Gratitude increases! This is exactly why I dedicate an entire chapter in this book to the topic of gratitude. This is the seed which all the other PTG changes grow from.

5. You feel a deepening of your soul's purpose, spiritual growth, or belief in your higher power. This can be the most powerful of all PTG outcomes. Remember the story I shared about the mom, Mary, who invited me to see my brokenness as an opportunity to build expansion joints? I believe it's in the sifting of all those broken pieces that we find our truest self and if we'd never been broken we'd never have found these nuggets.

Each of the five core elements I've shared in this book—wellness and self-care, letting go, love, connection, and gratitude—are the action steps and the pillars you need to lean in to the concept of PTG and find your empowered purpose as a result of your loss. You will find your empowered purpose when you do two things.

First, begin to map your life and explore what work needs to be done in each of the five pillars. Remember that these are not stages you work through, but rather each can meet you where you are now *and* later, depending on what's happening with your healing in the current moment. Sometimes you might be digging into two or three pillars; other times, you might find it necessary to focus on just one.

For example, as I write this part of the book, I'm finding that it's time for me to peel back another layer of letting go. I am feeling an internal battle of hanging on to thoughts that no longer serve me and are beginning to make me feel stuck, and how those are making other areas of my life difficult. As I sit with those thoughts, I find I am tapping into my inner wisdom from Chapter 5 to help me clarify what's important to me and how to move forward that is in alignment with my empowered purpose. And there's even a little bit of tapping into the wellness chapter as I find myself needing to move my body to help shake loose the thoughts that aren't clear—yet!

Second, get to know your grief intimately; acknowledge that it will grow and change just like a young child changes and the work you give your grief is appropriate for where you are along the path. Along with understanding that your grief is fluid and ever changing, you make sure that you give it a seat at the table with the other parts of you that make you the incredible divine human being that you are.

Part of my process right now is making sure that the job I'm giving my grief is still appropriate for its current stage. My grief no longer requires constant attention, nor does it have the energy of a rebellious teenager. It has matured and evolved into a more intimate relationship. This means that it's time for me to shift how I co-exist with it. If I don't, then I risk losing the work I've done up to this point.

I recently spoke at a national conference for parents who'd lost a child. I asked the people in my session how far out from their loss they were. I had one women who was less than six months and another woman who was over 22 years. As you know, I don't believe time heals all wounds—only action heals us—but I do feel like those two individuals should be experiencing two very different types of grief.

When I first started researching PTG, I assumed it was just a fancy term for resilience, meaning the ability to bounce back, time and time again, when life gives you lemons. But PTG is more than bouncing "back," because there is no going back to who you are after a loss. PTG means bouncing to the unknown, into levels of goodness you maybe didn't even know about. Resilience might enable you to bounce back but PTG allows you to bounce back HIGHER! So, let's think of it this way: if resilience is making lemonade out of lemons, PTG is makes a gourmet lemon chiffon cheesecake out of those same lemons (and after you've made the lemonade!).

This is where I get to combine the science with the woo-woo. PTG gives us an opportunity to deepen our roots into our soul's purpose. It allows us to connect to the divine and appreciate this one, wonderful, special life we still get to live.

My whole life, I've been resilient. I've bounced back from many adverse and traumatic experiences. But it wasn't until I expanded into how I could apply a deeper, more meaningful message to my suffering that I began to feel happier, more at peace, and in better alignment with my true purpose in life. Which is why I want share what I've learned and inspire others to be an active participant in their grief and create a beautiful life after loss.

I don't want for you to simply reach the previous level of functioning you were at before your loss. I want you to believe you can go beyond that point and actually thrive at a level beyond existing with a wound from losing a loved one. When you believe that you are capable of leaning in to this experience, you open an entire new world of possibility.

Let me share some wisdom that comes from living in a house full of boys. What do Batman and Spiderman have in common? The obvious answer is super powers and using them to make the world a better place. The not so obvious answer is that both of them were forever changed by the loss of a loved one, and they did this by accepting that although their life could never be what it once was, they could harness the potential of this brokenness into something totally different. That potential— the chance to see what you can accomplish on your own— wouldn't be available to them without the loss of their loved one.

The point I am trying to make is that even before there was research to prove PTG existed, human beings have recognized the potential power that develops from painful experiences. Consider this your personal invitation to wear a cape and find your superpowers!

Perhaps you don't live in the world of superheroes like I do, so let's look at some other people who've made radical, positive changes because of a traumatic event.

INSPIRING STORIES

The pink ribbon is so commonly associated with the Susan B. Komen Foundation. Breast cancer awareness began because Susan's sister wanted to find a cure for what killed her sister.

Candy Lightner founded Mothers Against Drunk Driving (MADD) after her daughter was killed by a drunk driver.

169

The No Notoriety campaign challenges the media not to publicize the names or photos of the murderers in mass killings; this campaign was in response to a family who lost a son in a mass shooting.

All of these organizations are the heart-based passion projects from people who've experienced tragic circumstances. These grieving people took all the pieces of their broken hearts and rebuilt them into movements that changed the landscape of how you and I think about breast cancer, drunk driving, and publicizing mass murderers. These people might not be caped crusaders in the traditional sense, but they have sure used their powers for good and changed the world for the better.

In Chapter 4, I asked you to explore how you are going to give your grief a job worthy of the love you feel for the person you've lost. The examples I've shared above are jobs those people gave their grief and how they choose to keep the memory of their loved one alive.

You don't have to do something as big as starting an organization that becomes a culture-shifting movement. Perhaps your super power is in the simple act of being a kinder and more compassionate human being.

My friend Shonna who I shared about in Chapter 5 has gone on to pursue her passion of adventure photography, taking pictures of people white water rafting and zip lining. She even spent a summer in Alaska as a photographer. And most recently, she took a class to become a victim's advocate in her community. These are the ways she is putting her grief to work and opportunities she couldn't see until she tapped into the growth potential grief offers us.

This is not an opportunity that any of us wish to have, but we do have this experience of loss and we should not waste it by letting our lives wither in the shadow of our loved one's death.

SEEING THE WORLD THROUGH FRESH EYES

I heard the story of a man who lost the love of his life to ovarian cancer. Lost in his grief for months and months, he knew he had to do something to change—or he would run the risk of never getting any part of himself back. He decided to take a canoe trip to the Yukon.

While on the trip, he had a near-death experience with a capsized canoe. He was stuck holding onto a rock in the running rapids for hours until a rescue team arrived. For months prior, he stated that though he wasn't suicidal, he didn't necessarily care to be living anymore, either. This experience of nearly dying in the rapids shook him and his grief to the core, and gave him the awareness that yes, he did want to live—and he wanted to live for something besides his grief.

This man chose not to let his near-death experience limit him from adventure in life; instead, it allowed him to pursue it. About nine months later, he had the experience of going on a rafting trip through the Grand Canyon. During this time, he spent every day with people who had started a franchise business. This man was a successful entrepreneur during his career, but he had retired when his wife became ill. In listening to these franchise owners, he felt a familiar excitement and passion sparking in him that he had not felt for years. He ended up buying a franchise and going into business with his son. Four years later, the franchise was successful and thriving, and it brought much goodness and gratitude to the man's life.

His loss and grief gave him a new opportunity to see the world with fresh eyes, and it opened him up to opportunities he wouldn't have had otherwise. It's important to acknowledge that this new goodness didn't come *because* of his loss, but because his loss created wildfires that burned his structures to the ground; instead of living forever in the charred landscape, he made the choice to rebuild.

None of us will ever have an answer for why loss happened to us, but we don't need to know the why in order to live a full life. We assume that knowing the why would make it better, but the reality is the why doesn't change the outcome—it doesn't bring your loved one back. Even if you knew the why, you would still miss your loved one and you would **still** have to do the work to heal. You would still have to take ownership of your healing journey and integrate this into your life's experience.

What Goes Up Must Go Down…and Back Up Higher

This life-changing experience that you are undergoing will not be the last time the universe gives you an AFGO. The purpose of our life is not to create, structure, plan, and live a life void of struggles and hardship. I believe the purpose of these experiences is to give us the opportunity to deepen our roots into the true essence of who are and how we're meant to shine our gifts into the world.

Unfortunately, we go to great lengths to avoid any discomfort, no matter how small or big. We live in environments that are perfectly climate controlled (not too hot, not too cold), everyone is a winner, and we avoid discomfort or disappointment at all costs. We are encouraged to be happy and accept that "everything happens for a reason," but the truth is, as you've experienced with your grief, the pendulum only swings as far to the left as you let it swing to the right.

Our growth as unique individuals is meant to go in both directions. And as much as we would prefer that our lives only have an upward trajectory, we are only able to reach the highest levels of self-worth and purpose when we embrace both the light and the dark.

The majority of our lives are lived in the space between the highest high and the lowest low. The larger we can make that space, the deeper our satisfaction is with our total life, which is why we must embrace, wholeheartedly, these AFGOs as invitations from Spirit to allow the darkness to swallow us up. We do this knowing that we will find our way through and come out into the sunshine as better, more authentic versions of ourselves. When we do that, we build our resilience muscles.

When I was about nine or ten, I got a trampoline for my birthday. When I first started bouncing on it, I couldn't go very high, but the more I learned to push down into the black mat of the trampoline I found that I could soar higher! So high sometimes that at the top of the bounce, my body would involuntarily wiggle with the fear of losing control at either end of the jump. I would then pull back on how much I pressed into the mat, which would lower the height of my jump. The fun and exhilaration of the highest bounces weren't a result of what happened above the trampoline mat; the lighthearted fun and tickle in my stomach was a result of how willing I was to push down into the resistance of the mat.

I beg you to be so brave as to push into the darkness that is below the surface of your comfort. Allow this hard work of healing from loss to rebound you to heights that make you giggle with joy, a joy that you would never have experienced had you not been so daring.

Your journey is just beginning. Hold on, dear one, for you never know where it will take you.

ACKNOWLEDGMENTS

There is no way for me to recognize, in any order, my gratitude for the people who've stood by me since Brandon's death. Each person has filled a unique and necessary role in my healing. Without each of these people this book would never have happened. So, I'll start with the one person who made this all possible.

Brandon I believe this book is a major part of your life's purpose. You always had a heart of gold that you wore on your sleeve (which you hated). That unguarded love and loyalty is now bringing healing into the world through this book and helping so many others find a way forward through love and loss.

Daniel, my wise old soul, I have learned so much from you and continue to admire the way in which you live your life. So often you were my life raft the first year after Brandon died. Some of my only good memories of that first year were the times I felt I had you to lean on and we shared our healing journey as we worked through our grief.

Jason there is no one along this entire journey who's carried a heavier load than you. You have sacrificed so much so that I and the rest of your family could thrive. The connection you and I have is a result of hard times and similarities in our personalities.

I cherish this connection and know the best is yet to come for you.

My little Sam - You are pure joy! Being able to share my memories of Brandon with you has been such a gift in keeping those memories alive. Although you don't remember him, he is so much a part of who you are and will impact your entire life.

To my amazing husband, Scott. I literally would not be here to share this book if you hadn't held everything together for me and our family. You did 100% of everything, for so long, I honestly don't know how you did it. And all while working nights and weekends. My love and gratitude for you goes far beyond an acknowledgement in a book. You have taught me the meaning of unconditional love and stood in the fire with me even when I did everything I could to make you leave. I can't imagine my life without you. I love you more.

There is no way to acknowledge my husband without recognizing his parents. Jim and Sally, you have shown me what family really means, which has healed decade-old wounds for me. Thank you for all you've done, it means more than you know.

In addition to Scott, Beth you too stood in the fire with me and never, not even once, winced when I lashed out at you. You are the embodiment of a High-High-Priestess! I feel so blessed to share the best and the worst of my life with you, and since you know ALL my secrets, I know we'll be friends for life.

To Dottie, my Saturday running partner for the past 16 years, the miles of life we've been through and the hills we've climbed have been easier with you at my side. The ground we've covered could fill another entire book. You are my running angel!

My childhood friend Helen. From the time I envied your gauchos in second grade you have been my soul sister. I know, whether we talk every day (like all through school) or once a year, we are never really separated. You know me in a way no one else does. I love you.

I also want to make sure that I sent out love to my Mom. Thank you for making me a resilient and strong woman and for giving me the freedom and independence to become who I am. I am so grateful you and Dad opened your home and adopted me.

To my community of Crazy Good Grief. You are my like-loss community; you are the ones who "get me." I've received so much healing from the energy and perspective of this group. You are the group I wish I had found in October 2010. Thank you for encouraging me and supporting my viewpoint on what it means to heal, even when it was hard to hear sometimes.

Lastly, to the amazing women who helped edit and made this book worthy of publication. Amy, of Wise Ink, thank you for believing in my vision and showing me how it could come to life. Carrie, of Typewriter Society, you took this book from good to great. Your input and word magic brought a book about death to life. Gillian, of GillianRyan Publishing, your final polish and attention to detail put the final shine on my book and made me proud to put it out into the world. Thank you all for your faith in me and recognizing the passion behind this project.

177

ABOUT THE AUTHOR

The death of her father as a teenager exposed Paula Stephens to a rudimentary education in what it feels like to grieve the loss of a loved one, but it was the unexpected death of her son, while home on leave from the Army in October of 2010 that shattered her life into pieces she thought she could never rebuild. On the five-year anniversary of Brandon's death, while at a yoga ashram in the Colorado Rocky Mountains, she reflected on the elements that allowed her to rebuild her broken heart. From the crisp fall Rocky Mountain air, this book was born.

Paula has become a nationally known speaker, yogi and blogger on the topic of grief, especially the difficult topic of child loss. Her blog titled 'What I Wish Other People Understood About

Losing A Child' has over 1.3 million views and continues to be a comfort and inspiration to parents around the world.

Paula has a Master's degree in Exercise Physiology and has previously taught at Metro State University in Denver. She is also a wellness coach and has taught yoga for the past 13 years. It was her 25 years in the health and wellness industry that made her realize the lack of mind-body support and awareness in the grief community. As a result, she teaches Yoga for Grief workshops and speaks at national events on the topic of the importance of wellness in the healing of grief.

She is a popular speaker at resilience and military loss events. She has also been a speaker at the National Resilience Institute Resilience Summit, The Compassionate Friends, and Life Source-Organ and Tissue Donation

Paula lives in Colorado with her remaining three adventuresome sons, two big dogs and one incredible husband. You can find her on a mountain bike, trail run, ski slope or yoga mat throughout the year as she uses the power of nature to heal and remind her of what an incredible life she still has to live.

END NOTES

1. Barks, Coleman. *The Essential Rumi*. New York: Harper Collins, 1997.

2. Kübler-Ross, Elisabeth. *On Death and Dying*. New York: Scribner, 2011.

3. Ibid.

4. Barks, *The Essential Rumi*.

5. Schwartz, R. C. *Internal Family Systems Therapy*. New York: Guilford Publications, 1995.

6. Chapman, Gary D. *The Five Love Languages: How to Express Heartfelt Commitment to Your Mate*. Chicago: Northfield Pub., 1995.

7. Barks, *The Essential Rumi*.

8. Dass, Ram, and Rameshwar Das. *Polishing the Mirror: How to Live from Your Spiritual Heart*. Boulder, CO: Sounds True, 2013.

9. Van Der Kolk, Bessel. *The Body Keeps the Score: Brain, Mind, Body in the Healing of Trauma*. New York: Penguin Books, 2014.

10. Ratey, John J. *Spark: The Revolutionary New Science of Exercise and the Brain*. New York: Little Brown, 2012.

11. Mostofsky, E., J. B. Sherwood, M. A. Mittleman, M. Maclure, G. H. Tofler, and J. E. Muller. "Response to Letter Regarding Article, 'Risk of Acute Myocardial Infarction After the Death of a Significant Person in One's Life: The Determinants of Myocardial Infarction Onset Study'" *Circulation* 126.3 (2012).

12. Maslow, A. H. "A Theory of Human Motivation." *Psychological Review*, 50 (1943): 370-96.

13. Ratey, *Spark*.

14. Barks, *The Essential Rumi.*

15. Brown, Brené. *The Gifts of Imperfection: Let Go of Who You Think You're Supposed to Be and Embrace Who You Are*. Center City, MN: Hazelden. 2010.

16. Ibid.

17. Brown, Brené. *Rising Strong: The Reckoning. The Rumble. The Revolution*. New York: Spiegel & Grau, 2015.

18. Young, William P. *The Shack: Where Tragedy Confronts Eternity*. Newbury Park, CA: Windblown Media, 2007.

19. Brown, *Rising Strong*.

20. Strayed, Cheryl. *Wild: A Journey from Lost to Found*. New York: Knopf, 2012.

21. Breathnach, Sarah Ban. *Simple Abundance: A Daybook of Comfort and Joy*. New York: Warner, 1995.

22. Powell, Toni. "A Love Story: Toni Powell at TEDxNoosa." Perf. *TEDx Talks*, 11 May 2013. Web.

23. Hanson, Rick, and Richard Mendius. *Buddha's Brain: The Practical Neuroscience of Happiness, Love & Wisdom*. Oakland, CA: New Harbinger Publications, 2009.

24. Kang, Hyo Jung, Bhavya Voleti, Tibor Hajszan, Grazyna Rajkowska, Craig A Stockmeier, Pawel Licznerski, Ashley Lepack, Mahesh S Majik, Lak Shin Jeong, Mounira Banasr, Hyeon Son, Ronald S Duman. "Decreased expression of synapse-related genes and loss of synapses in major depressive disorder." *Nature Medicine*, 18 (2012). doi:10.1038/nm.2886.

25. Emmons, Robert A. and Michael E. Mccullough. "Counting Blessings versus Burdens: An Experimental Investigation of Gratitude and Subjective Well-being in Daily Life." *Journal of Personality & Social Psychology* 84.2 (2003): 377-89.

26. Ibid.

27. Dass, *Polishing the Mirror*.

28. Tedeschi, R. G. and L. G. Calhoun. *Trauma & Transformation: Growing in the Aftermath of Suffering*. Thousand Oaks, CA: Sage Publications, 1995.

$$15,000$$
$$+\ 80,000$$
$$\overline{\ 95,000}$$
$$+\ 60,000$$
$$\overline{\ 155,000}$$

Made in the USA
San Bernardino, CA
08 January 2017